MAYDAY!

A Physician As Patient

ALLAN LOHAUS, M.D.

MAYDAY!
PUBLISHED BY SYNERGY BOOKS
2100 Kramer Lane, Suite 300
Austin, Texas 78758

For more information about our books, please write to us, call 512.478.2028, or visit our website as www.bookpros.com.

ISBN-10: 0-9755922-9-7
ISBN-13: 978-0-9755922-9-8

Publisher's Cataloging-in-Publication
(Provided by Quality Books, Inc.)

Lohaus, Allan William.
    Mayday! : a physician as patient / Allan Lohaus.
    p. cm.
    Includes index.
    LCCN 2005926639
    ISBN-13: 978-0-9755922-9-8
    ISBN-10: 0-9755922-9-7

    1. Lohaus, Allan William. 2. Physicians—Maryland—Biography. 3. Physician and patient. 4. Patients—Psychology. I. Title.

        R154.L563A3 2006   610'.92
                            QBI05-600060

10 9 8 7 6 5 4 3 2 1

For my mother who taught me courage.

CONTENTS

PART ONE

SHIPWRECK

On a muggy summer evening, standing at the helm of our sailboat *Second Chance*, I steer an overnight race from Annapolis to St. Mary's. In a steady breeze, full sails drive her dark-green hull easily through light, choppy waves. The stern wake hisses as lights twinkle on other vessels as well as on the shores.

As we pass Thomas Point Light, the gray sky abruptly darkens as low, black clouds rush in from the west. I smell ozone on the building wind and I hear distant thunder. Suddenly, lightning bolts zigzag across the sky. Then, rain and hail pelt us. Frantically, the crew pulls down the sails. A great gust knocks us onto our port side. Wind and spray roar over ten-foot swells. Giant furious waves crash on the deck, washing the crew overboard. Water rushes into the cockpit and through the companionway to the cabin below.

"MAYDAY! MAYDAY! MAYDAY!" I shout as the sloop sinks beneath me.

My shouts end the dream. I awake alone in an isolation room on the eleventh floor of Boston's Brigham and Women's Hospital. Pale winter sunlight filters through the curtained window wall. Flowers on the window sill fragrance the room with freesia, my favorite second only to my wife's perfume, Anaïs Anaïs. More fresh flowers arrive almost

9

daily with notes containing heartfelt wishes, comfort, and love.

On this morning in February 1999, the third month of my illness, I have not eaten or drunk anything for thirteen weeks. I weigh fifty pounds less than normal. My looks frighten me: my ribs and sternum protrude; little muscle remains in my neck, left arm, and shoulders; all large muscles are considerably smaller. Most of my head and body hair has fallen out. The backs of my hands are bruised brown and blue. As my fingers have become white and thin, my wedding ring slips off too easily, and my wife Martha wears it on a necklace.

Motors hum. One pumps intravenous (IV) fluids and antibiotics, another total parenteral nutrition (TPN) and other medications into me through a peripherally inserted central catheter, or PICC line, which is a sterile tube entering a vein in my left inner arm above the elbow and extending to the right chamber of my heart. Another motor pumps a feeding solution into me through a tube halfway down the left side of my abdomen. Yet another pressurizes the mattress on which I lay. Alarms beep as antibiotics and IVs finish or as the pumps malfunction. Sometimes the high-pitched triple beeps continue many minutes until the nurses come to my bedside to rectify the event. The overhead paging in the hallway is muffled unless a fire, security emergency, or cardiac arrest requires hospital-wide response. When that happens, the voices proclaiming, "CODE RED!" "CODE WHITE!" or "CODE BLUE!" disturb even the hard-of-hearing behind closed doors. This morning I am anxious and disturbed by the dream and the racing of my tired and tireless mind. Critically ill, I want to live.

As I lay in my bed, questions race through my mind. Is my life over? How will it end? Coma? Hemorrhage? Infection? What really was done during the first surgery? Was the postop care too casual? Did I take too little responsibility for my care? What will it take to heal the small-bowel perforation? How long will the internal infections persist? Will I survive the needed third operation? Will I again practice gynecology? I sigh, close my eyes, and try to imagine how Martha and the children will cope if I die. What *will* happen if I die? Will there be a dark tunnel ending in bright light? Will I see my parents on the other side? Should I be cremated? Where will I be buried? Was the dream an omen?

I force myself to take a deep breath and start my morning prayer, "Mother, Father, creating God, you accompany me in all my efforts."

Rising on swells of optimism, tugged down by undertows of pain and infection, I drift through waters too dark for me to see hidden dangers, waters too deep in which to stand. The intestinal perforation and complications I have been dealing with has disconnected me from my life as a person, husband, physician, father, family member, friend, and photographer. Energy wanes from my weakened body. Anxiety floods over me.

Day sixty-seven begins.

EARLIER VOYAGES

During my late adolescence in the 1950s, episodes of abdominal pain and indigestion began and continued intermittently. For one episode, a rural general practitioner prescribed an enema and told me, "If you're not better tomorrow, I'll take out your appendix. I've just been certified for that operation." That night the enema and prayers worked.

In the decades since, when I have had abdominal pains I diagnosed and treated myself. I avoided caffeine, chocolate, citrus, soda, peppermint, alcohol, and fried foods. I selected from a menu of antacids, milk, Pepto Bismol tablets and liquid, acid blockers, Axid, Tagamet, Pepcid, and Prilosec. Then, in January 1998, the words of Dr. William Osler, a giant of American medicine, spoke to me. Remembering words from his *Aphorisms,* which I had read as an intern, I recalled, "A physician who treats himself has a fool for a patient." I decided I would no longer be my own physician.

A fine gastroenterologist practiced in our New Hampshire town of Wolfeboro. He evaluated, diagnosed, and managed my symptoms of heartburn, indigestion, and regurgitation from irritation of the esophagus and stomach. After three months of treatment, he performed an upper-digestive-tract endoscopy, an examination using a flexible fiber-optic instrument to visualize the tissues and biopsy the abnormalities. Rare-type polyps were found in the small intestine (benign villous adenomas), having about a ten-percent likelihood of becoming malignant. A second endoscopic procedure to remove the growths was followed three months later by yet another endoscopy to see if the problem was resolved. However, the polyps had returned to full size, requiring abdominal surgery. The gastroenterologist and a general surgeon conferred.

As a practicing gynecologist I had operated with this general surgeon, each assisting on the other's cases, for the past four years . He was skilled, thoughtful, and careful; I trusted him. During a brief preoperative consultation, he provided Martha and me with additional information. The procedure, an opening of the abdomen (exploratory laparotomy) and removal of the polyps from the small intestine (duodenotomy and excisional biopsies), were discussed. The benefits were understood and the risks outlined: infections, blood loss, bowel obstruction, and possible injury to other organs. The operation would be performed November 29, 1998.

As a physician about to be a patient, I thought about how I had become a doctor.

My journey began with an interest in physical therapy when I was a high school senior in White Plains, New York in 1960. I visited the physical therapy department at Columbia University Hospital in New York City. The machines, starched uniforms, and the aromas combined to make it a perfect place. I wanted to be a professional working to help others be healthy.

Later, during the summer following my freshman year at Earlham College in Indiana, I worked as an extern at the Burke Foundation Rehabilitation Hospital in White Plains, New York. Three other college externs and I shared the tasks of transporting patients to physical therapy, occupational therapy, and other activities by wheelchair and stretcher; we gave bed baths, made beds, fed patients, and assisted the nurses and therapists. We wore white uniforms and I dreamed of my future in this helping profession. At the end of that summer, the others returned to their premed studies and I returned to Earlham to begin my sophomore year.

Back at college I thought, *I'm as bright and committed as they are, perhaps I can be premed.* Discussing this interest with my adviser, he agreed. "You have what it takes to be premed."

In October 1963, my junior year, while sitting and staring out my dormitory window, I watched pale leaves dance on the college lawns and walkways. Rocking gently, I closed my eyes and nervously stroked my eyebrows and forehead with my left thumb and fingers. My lips and mouth became dry. I had taken the Medical College Admissions Test five days ago and my thoughts were racing. How did I do? Am I smart enough? I've been on the Dean's list, but I didn't take calculus. I want to be a doctor—perhaps a pediatrician. I like children. Can I afford it? I'll be saving senior-year expenses. I'll need loans and part-time work and I can apply for scholarships. I'll cross that bridge . . . . If I get accepted, I'll find a way.

I turned away from the window and looked at a neat stack of manila folders containing applications and essays that sat on my desk. In my best handwriting, I began filling in the application for the George Washington University School of Medicine.

Ten days after mailing the application I made my daily visit to the campus post office. I passed the rows of square brass boxes, each with two knobs and a window. I bent slightly and peered through No. 262. Inside was a letter. I opened the box and took out a buff-colored envelope with a navy-blue return address: The George Washington University School of Medicine. Tucking it in the organic chemistry book under my left arm, I hurried across campus to the privacy of my room. A rejection? Too soon for an acceptance. What can it be? Unfolding it, I read:

"Dear Mr. Lohaus:

Our Committee on Admissions, before proceeding to its final evaluation of your credentials, wishes to extend to you an invitation to meet with a representative of the Committee.

Since it would be something of an imposition to ask you to make the trip to Washington, we ask that within the next week you get in touch with Dr. Carl P. Huber, 1040-1232 W. Michigan Street, Indianapolis, Indiana, to arrange an appointment.

We regard this interview as an important part of our evaluation procedures, and cannot have a final recommendation by the Committee until we receive our representative's comments.

Most sincerely yours,
Angus M. Griffin
Associate Dean"

At eleven-thirty in the morning on November 22, I climbed aboard a Trailways bus in Richmond, Indiana, for the one-and-a-half-hour trip to Indianapolis. Wearing my second-hand gray suit, white shirt, and thin blue tie, I was clean-shaven and grasped a tan raincoat in my left hand. The ride was uneventful through a constant drizzle. At the terminal when the bus door opened, newsboys shouted, "Extra! Extra! Read all about it! The president's been shot!"

"Oh my God!" I gasped.

Bus passengers cried and a woman behind me yelled, "I'd like to shake the hand that did it!" I could not look back at her. I hoped Kennedy wasn't badly wounded. Regardless, I had to get to the Indiana University Medical Center on time for my two o'clock appointment.

Opening the thick glass doors on Michigan Street, I crossed the marble entry hall to the information desk. Taking an elevator, I arrived at Dr. Huber's office twenty minutes early and sat in his empty waiting room. I knew that this interview would be an important part of the admission process. What will Dr. Huber be asking? What qualities is he looking for in me? What do other applicants have that I don't? I wiped my front teeth with my handkerchief, then checked my tie and my zipper.

At five after two, the door opened and a short, portly man in a white coat looked at me. "Mr. Lohaus?"

"Yes," I replied, standing up.

"I'm Dr. Huber, please come in." I followed him into his office. I scanned his floor-to-ceiling shelves filled with books and mementos and the many framed documents on the wall behind his large mahogany desk. In the center was his George Washington University Medical School diploma, surrounded by licenses, U.S. Army Hospital training certificates, a number of house staff pictures, awards, and Certification by the American Board of Obstetrics and Gynecology. As he approached his desk, he gestured at a chair for me. Sitting, I looked quickly at his serious face, at his shining bald head fringed with short, white hair, and at his blue eyes through his rimless glasses.

"You have heard the news?"

"Yes, Dr. Huber."

"Was your travel delayed?"

"No."

Looking down at the papers before him and then up at me, he

asked, "Why have you applied to the Medical School at George Washington?"

Focusing on the bridge of his nose, I spoke earnestly, "I feel called to be a physician. I want to prevent illness and preserve peoples' health. I would like the opportunity to study at George Washington because of its strengths in clinical medicine. I want to be a clinician."

"Is anyone in your family a physician?"

"No."

He seemed distracted, perhaps by the assassination attempt. Anxiously, I studied his face as he stood and extended his right hand across the desk. "Thank you for coming, Mr. Lohaus. You are a fine young man. I will contact Dr. Calabrisi about your interview." Releasing my hand, he escorted me to the waiting room.

Outside the medical center in the gray drizzle I hailed a cab. "I want to go to the bus station."

"Okay. You've heard Kennedy's been shot?"

"Yes. How's he doing?"

"It's serious." We listened to the taxi radio. Bulletins from Dallas reported the unfolding tragedy. At the bus station I stepped aboard the eastbound bus marked New York with a scheduled stop in Richmond.

In Richmond I got off the bus into a downpour. Pulling the raincoat collar up around my neck, I walked in the dark onto campus and into my room. The light was on and Tom, my roommate, looked up at me from his desk.

"Kennedy is dead." he told me sadly, yet gently.

"Oh, God, why? Who shot him?"

Tom shrugged. Nauseated and numb, I took off my wet clothes and crawled into bed under a blanket. I laid on my back, sad and confused, and stared at the underside of Tom's bunk above me.

Six months later, in early May 1964, my premed adviser, Dr. William Stephenson, greeted me as I left a biochemistry lecture. "Can you stop up in my office for a moment?"

"Sure."

He slipped behind his desk and we sat. I looked at his friendly, boyish face as he spoke. "We would like you to stay for commencement." He paused.

I thought, *But I'm not graduating yet.*

"You'll be receiving an award," he continued. "Your mother has been invited. Congratulations."

The June sun shone through oaks and maples surrounding Chase Stage. With my mother holding on to my arm, we walked to the second row in the audience and sat. The degrees were awarded and the presentation of awards followed. When the provost announced, "The Malcolm Pre-Medical Award is given by Dr. and Mrs. Russell L. Malcolm," I held my breath. "This award," the provost said, "goes to the premedical student whose excellence in science and general scholarship and whose character and mental attitude give promise of outstanding success as a physician. The recipient is . . . Allan Lohaus." Eagerly, I walked to the stage. President Bolling's eyes twinkled and he smiled broadly as he grasped and shook my hand. He extended his left hand with the award envelope and patted my shoulder. "Congratulations, Allan." I tingled, feeling flushed and numb. Filled with happiness, I was delighted, yet unsure about beginning my medical career.

DAY ONE

A NOVEMBER MORNING

The morning of surgery is both familiar and strange. I have been in hospital rooms since 1966, and in this particular rural New Hampshire hospital room, number 147, many times as a physician and surgeon. Now, at seven o'clock in the morning, I'm dressed only in a hospital gown, called a johnny, and lie under a sheet with a bracelet clipped on my right wrist that reads, *Dr. Allan Lohaus, patient.*

The other bed is empty. Sunlight fills the room through large windows. Debbie, a friendly nurse I've worked with for three years, wheels in the IV pole with a Ringer's lactate bag hanging on it and prepares to start the IV. I look away and focus on my breathing. I feel a painful stick and immediately look up at the burette on the IV bag to see how it is running. A few drops fall, then sputter, and stop. "I'm sorry, the vein moved," Debbie says. "I'll try again."

"No, let's let Dr. Ellis start it in the OR," I say. The site burns and swells. She applies a pressure dressing to prevent more swelling.

I hate and fear needles despite my years of medical training. This unsuccessful IV insertion adds to more than fifty years of needle traumas that have included polio shots, stitches when my left knee met barbed wire at age seven, and dental Novacaine once in childhood (but not again until topical gel to numb the injection site became available in my forties). The injection of a wart in the ball of my right foot was the worst pain I have ever had. When receiving a precollege tetanus booster, I felt faint and heard the nurse warn, "You're too big to catch." I came to on the floor. In medical school, students drew blood from each other for hematology labs. We sat alphabetically and Ira, to my right, had been a phlebotomist—a lab technician who draws blood—so I chose him and appreciated his skill.

"Please slide over onto the gurney," Debbie requests. Can I perform this delicate act wearing no underwear?

At the door to the operating room, my petite, brunette wife Martha takes my hand. I gaze into her beautiful brown eyes. "Muff, I love you, darling."

We share a tender kiss. "I love you, babe."

DAY TWO

AT ANCHOR

L ying in bed back in Room 147 with the IV fluids running, this is my first day ever as a hospitalized patient. The orange nasogastric tube, which runs through my nose to my stomach draining stomach fluids into a bottle, is taped to my nose and a catheter drains my bladder. My abdomen is sore. The dressing is dry. Mentally I'm doing my own postop evaluation. I seem to be stable.

I follow the instructions and push a button for pain medication that delivers it into my IV. This nauseates me and makes me groggy. My belly aches and I'm not sure I have slept. I hurt and feel anxious. Nursing activities go on around me. I can't remember what has happened. I am confused. But I know Martha is with me.

DAY THREE

NEAR DROWNING

My mind begins doing funny things on the third postop day. Sleep-deprived from pain and poor pain management, I have a limited, intermittent grip on reality. During the night I climbed over the bed rails, pulled out my IV, NG tube, and Foley catheter, and wandered into the ER, bleeding from the IV site and yelling, "I need help! The nursing care stinks! Get me out of here!"

I wonder how I got there unobserved.

Anxious and agitated, I urge my mind to take responsibility for my care. The medications seem to intensify the delirium. Blood tests show a critically low level of calcium, 6.9. "That can't be correct, I'd be dead," I say to the nurse. The retest indicates laboratory error.

Coughing and feverish, I am sent for an X-ray that confirms early pneumonia. I have an adverse reaction to respiratory therapy that causes me to wheeze and increases my already labored breathing. The nurse starts oxygen. While I am resting fitfully, the paging system frequently barks over my head, startling me and ending moments of rest.

On the fourth postop day I am transferred to a windowless ICU room. The same hour brings moments of clarity and confusion. I am a patient, a doctor, a fleeing fugitive.

"Nurse, can I have some water?"

"It isn't ordered for you."

"I'm so thirsty, so hot, please get me a drink. Please, I need a drink."

I get nothing for a while. Finally, the nurse reappears. "You can have sips of water." With the straw to my lips, I draw an ice-cold sip. Then I suck as hard as I can, filling my mouth and swallowing. She withdraws the straw from my mouth and places the cup out of my reach. Later, I awake with my tongue sticking to the roof of my mouth, my parched lips swollen and cracking. I speak with difficulty in a tired whisper. "Nurse, I need a drink . . . I need food . . . I'm getting weaker. Please help me."

"Only sips of water for now. I'll check with the doctor."

She returns bringing cranberry juice. "The doctor said you can have anything you want." I gulp the cup of juice. Asking for another cup, I gulp that. I feel hot, tired, and nauseated. I should not be drinking. If I weren't a physician, how would my care be managed? Being a physician is a curse.

A CT scan—a computerized X-ray test—reveals bubbles at the intestinal operative site, probable evidence of leakage and infection. The general surgeon and his associate have differing opinions as to the seriousness of this development. My status is critical with diagnoses of pancreatitis, pneumonia, probable small-bowel perforation, and ICU psychosis. Antibiotics and antianxiety medicines are being administered. Demerol is discontinued and morphine started. The IV sites become infiltrated and are abandoned; each new one more painful to start than the last. Precious few veins remain.

Spiking fevers start with my temperature over 102. A cooling blanket under me lowers my temperature below 101.

The director of medical social work visits Martha and asks, "Do you want him here in the ICU?" A physician friend then confides to her, "They may have done all they can here and Allan should be transferred." The surgeon later confirms what my physician friend had said. "We are in over our heads," he says to Martha. "Allan needs to be transferred. You can take him anywhere you wish."

The following day the CT scan confirms a perforation of the duodenum and the surgeon tells me, "This is bad news."

The back pain worsens from infection between my organs and my back. The surgeon offers me a transfer to another rural hospital with an endoscopic surgical fellow. "He may be able to close the perforation."

"No, I think I better go to Boston."

He leaves. I am alone. He has not offered to get me to Boston.

"I am going to die here unless I arrange for a transfer," I tell no one and everyone.

During the years of practicing gynecology in New Hampshire, I have consulted with gynecologists at Boston's Brigham and Women's Hospital. I call one and tell him, "Ray, I'm between a rock and a hard place. I need to be admitted to a general surgeon. Who would you have take care of you if you had duodenal perforation, peritonitis, pneumonia, and pancreatitis?"

"Dr. David Brooks," Ray says.

Later in the afternoon, Dr. Brooks speaks with Martha. I can be transferred to his service the next day at ten o'clock in the morning. Relieved that I will be transferred, I rest, then sleep.

I awake confused and can't find the nurse call button, so I call out, "Nurse what time is it? I want to go home."

"You can't go home."

Pulling myself to the right-side bed rails, I lift my left foot and rest it on the top rung.

"Better lie on your back." She pulls the sheet up to my chin. "Try to rest." For a while I lie quietly then I feel choked by the oxygen mask. I am anxious about suffocating. I pull off the mask with my left hand, my right arm being held rigidly on an arm board to protect the IV. The alarm rings because my oxygen level is too low. The nurse comes back to my bedside.

"I'm being choked by the mask." She replaces the mask with nasal cannulas—small tubes in each nostril. The agitation passes. I pray that I will live until transferred. I pray that Dr. Brooks will save my life. I am not afraid of death. I am unsure I will live.

I close my eyes. I see myself at age four climbing the wooden stairs from the kitchen to the second floor of my childhood home. I wear my mother's apron and hold a plate of orange slices with my right hand. My clenched left hand rests in the apron pocket. Knocking on my parent's bedroom door they tell me to come in and I enter to see their smiling faces from their bed.

"Thank you," they say. I smile too.

"Why is your hand in the pocket?" Mommy asks.

"I cut myself."

"Come here let me see it," she says. She holds a tissue to it and kisses my forehead. I climb up and sit between them on the bed. Together we eat the orange slices.

Another scene follows: I am ten and pump myself on a swing hanging on the apple tree in our backyard near the garage. Suddenly my father shouts and curses in his garage carpentry shop. He runs to the house holding his hand. I jump from the swing and run after him, passing the open shop door. I hear the power saw still running. I follow him through the kitchen door. I hear his moans from the living room. He is lying on the couch; my mother kneels next to him holding his bandana-wrapped hand.

"Daddy hurt his hand when a piece of wood shot back from the saw," Mommy says. I leave the room and go to the bathroom. Wetting a washcloth with cold water, I bring it and put it on his forehead. He reaches up and throws the cloth to the floor with a curse. I leave the room confused and sad.

When I awake, it is warm in bed, and wet. I am lying in stool. "Nurse, I need some help." The nurse bathes me and asks rhetorically, "Why do the doctors order the medicine that does this?" This patient who is a doctor has no answer.

The nursing staff changes. Morning! A few more hours until transfer to Boston.

A glitch! No transfer until a bed is available, which will probably be after morning discharges at eleven o'clock. With my temperature at 102.8, the nurse again switches on the cooling blanket.

At eleven-thirty, Brigham won't give an admission number and the ambulance transfer must be postponed. Panicky, I call a gynecologic oncologist at Brigham, to see if he will release one of his beds for me. He is in the operating room and will call back when available. The ambulance company will come as late as two-thirty in the afternoon, but not later. Prayers fill the moments. Mike, a family friend, prepares an egg-crate mattress for a more comfortable ambulance-stretcher ride as I wait for the call. My nurse calls Brigham at one-fifteen. Politely, she asks for the admission number as part of the transfer preparation. She gets it. I am going!

The ambulance arrives at two P.M. The paperwork and MasterCard payment take thirty minutes. Wrapped in blankets over an adult diaper and scrub suit, I am taken through the ER to the frigid ambulance. The stretcher is locked to the inside walls. I shiver violently against the straps. Driving south, I rise and fall and rise again. I am anxious and become confused. Are those hills and valleys or ocean swells? I hear sirens. From the ambulance or Coast Guard vessels? Am I alive or drowning? Am I being rescued?

PART TWO

PART TWO

DAY NINE

RESCUE

Martha stands at the foot of my new bed in Boston as my stretcher docks next to it. Her tired face and dark-ringed eyes smile as I am transferred into the bed. She kisses my face and strokes my hair into place. "We made it," she says softly.

Pains stab through my abdomen. I start shivering, then shaking. "I need pain medicine."

"I'll get the nurse," Martha responds. A nurse with bright red hair comes in.

"I need pain medicine."

"The intern and resident will order it after they evaluate you."

"Please call them and tell them I'm really hurting."

"I'll call them now."

With each harsh cough, I have the worst pain yet. I groan loudly.

The oxygen cannulas press inside my burning nostrils. Anxious, I ask myself questions. How many liters of oxygen am I getting? When will the doctors come? How soon will the fever be controlled? When will my mind clear?

After evaluation and medication, blood is drawn; many vials, too many to count. The man in the next bed coughs and moans, then mumbles in an eastern European language.

Sometime after eight that evening, Dr. Brooks enters. A man my age, he is tall, with sandy hair, tortoiseshell glasses, and a friendly and confident look. He wears a white coat over a blue oxford button-down-collar shirt and a snappy, striped navy tie. He is a doctor's doctor. I'm in his care at last. I hope he can stop the fevers and help my intestine to heal. He tells me he may have to operate. I look at his hands. They are smaller than I expected for a man his size but look strong, with clean, neatly trimmed nails and a gold wedding band on his left ring finger. *Help me*, I think. *Save my life.*

DAY TEN

PRIVATE QUARTERS

L ying on an X-ray table, I pray, "God, guide his hands," as the interventional radiologist places a drain through my right flank. The prayer, a gift to me as a surgeon years before, had come from a patient of mine. Holding her hand as preparations for her anesthetic had begun, I had asked, "Any last questions or concerns before anesthesia?"

"No. God will guide your hands," she had assured me. As I scrubbed for her operation and hundreds that followed, I always prayed as I scrubbed, "God, guide my hands."

I repeat the prayer continuously during the half hour the radiologist manipulates a fifteen-inch wire covered by a minuscule tube to reach the infected tissue near my right kidney. When he is satisfied with the placement, he withdraws the wire, secures the drain to my skin and attaches a suction bulb to the tube.

Two days after the drain placement, the testing of the fluid reveals germs including *Staphylococcus aureus* (staph), usually treated with a penicillin derivative, methicillin. The staph from my infection turns out to be the methicillin-resistant type and requires isolation procedures to prevent the spread to other patients and hospital personnel. I am moved into an isolation room and everyone who comes in contact with me will wear gloves, a cover gown, and a mask.

The fevers with migraines continue in private quarters.

Late in the afternoon my physician, Dr. Peter Banks, ten years my senior, enters and sits on the foot of my bed. He towers over me, a giant of a man, a giant of a physician. My life is in his hands and those of Dr. Brooks, my surgeon. Our eyes meet. "Dr. Lohaus," he says. "I wish I could make you well in a few days. But, with what you've been dealt, that can't happen. The perforation has not healed. You will be well again, but it will take time. Maybe months."

As Dr. Banks stands to leave, his smile lines deepen. "I'll be with you through this. My home number is on the back of my card. Call me any time."

I wonder about how he became a physician then remember an important day in my becoming a physician. The morning of February 3, 1964, I had gone to the college post office after my ten o'clock class. I pulled out envelopes from my box that included a thin, buff-colored one with a familiar navy-blue return address from George Washington. *Acceptances are thick*, I thought to myself, *because they come with commitment letters to be returned.* My letter seemed too thin. Quickly I stepped into an alcove, leaned against the wall, and opened the envelope. Unfolding the single page, my hands trembled as I read:

"Dear Mr. Lohaus:

I am happy to inform you that the Committee on Admissions has approved your application for admission to the first-year class beginning in September 1964. An official letter of acceptance will soon follow . . ."

"Yes!" I exclaimed happily to the world. "I'm in."

Elated, I walked briskly to the student commons to call my mother on a public phone. "Hi, Mom. I've been accepted at George Washington."

"Oh, Allan, that's wonderful. I'm so proud of you," Mom replied.

With my parents divorced, I decided to wait until evening to call my father in New York so that he would be at home. When the time came, I felt anxious approaching the phone. I hadn't spoken to him in months. I hadn't responded to his monthly letters, which were often moralistic and critical, and always filled with advice. Yet, I wanted to tell him. I hoped for affirmation. I dialed and listened.

"Hallo." I recognized his sad voice and German accent.

"Hello, Dad. This is Allan."

"Vere are you?"

"I'm at college." I started to tremble. "I'm calling you to tell you that I've been accepted to medical school."

"You have. That's vat you vant to do?"

"Yes, I'll be starting in September."

No response. A long silence passed. Then he said, "You know doctors are quacks."

Shaken, I replied, "I don't think I'll be a quack. I want to practice pediatrics . . . take care of children and educate parents."

"I haven't heard from you in a long time. Did you get my letters?"

"I did Dad . . . . Goodbye." Trembling, sweating, and wanting to vomit, I walked out into the cold. Why did I waste the money? *No matter what I do*, I thought, *it's never good enough for him.*

DAY THIRTEEN

SURPRISE

A CT scan is scheduled today for one o'clock in the afternoon but ends up being delayed repeatedly until seven by hospital emergencies. Starting at six-thirty, I drink a quart of salty, bitter X-ray contrast liquid. Now it's eight-thirty and still no call to come to the X-ray department. I dread drinking more when called. A nurses' aide comes into the room repeatedly to check on me. I am too tired to open my eyes with her comings and goings, yet I'm puzzled. What is there to check? Finally, at nine-thirty the stretcher from X-ray arrives and the aide assists with my transfer. She pulls down the sheet and pushes my pajama shirt into my pajama pants and grasps my penis in her ungloved fingers and moves it down deeper into the pants. Shocked by this inappropriate touching I feel so violated by this unprofessional act. I look up and see the back of her head as she turns away and walks out of the room. Were any of my hospitalized patients touched inappropriately? Will I report it? I'll decide later.

DAY FOURTEEN

A STAR

Ongoing fevers with migraines and lack of sleep exhaust me. A nurse comes into my room for morning care. I don't know her name.

"Nurse, I want to talk to a psychiatrist."

"There is a psychiatrist specializing in illness as a life crisis. I'll call his office in the hospital."

The next morning, sitting facing me, Dr. Gregory appears to be in his mid-forties and is tall, robust, and handsome, with smiling eyes and an expressive face. His vitality brings good energy into the room.

"I feel fragile . . . really fragile, emotionally." I pause, fighting back tears. "The fevers are really getting to me. The migraines with them are the worst pain I've had during this illness. I put an ice bag on my head. I ask for Percocet by injection. The relief lasts up to an hour. Then, a few hours later, another spike and I go through it again. When I was admitted here the medicine I took for migraines and depression was stopped. Could you order something to help me?"

He smiles. He understands without pity. We discuss options for medicines and he says he will order them today.

At Brigham, consultants' orders are entered into the pharmacy computer by the interns. At eight o'clock that night I ask for the sleeping medicine by name and the nurse tells me, "The intern ordered something else."

35

"I need to talk with the intern."

"She is in surgery until ten."

"I'll talk with her then."

"Do you want me to call her in the OR?"

"Yes. Tell her I want the medicine Dr. Gregory ordered. He has years of experience and he has reasons for this choice." The intern is called in the operating room. She agrees to Dr. Gregory's choice and will enter the order in the computer system when out of surgery. At eleven-thirty the sleeping medicine arrives.

During my own internship in 1968, a ringing telephone woke me most nights I was on duty. I remember one in particular.

"Doctor Lohaus?" the voice said when I picked up the phone.

"Yes."

"This is the nurse on pediatrics. The patient in room 232 has died. Will you come and pronounce her dead?"

"Yes, I'll be right there." Sitting up, I pulled on my shoes, and standing, I put on my white jacket over the green scrub suit I slept in.

Trudging through the long tunnel to the hospital, my mind cleared as I reviewed the protocol for pronouncing a patient: Place my stethoscope over the heart and listen for heartbeats…then move it over each lung to hear any breath sounds…feel the carotid arteries in the neck for pulses… then open the eyelids and check the pupils with a flashlight.

Michelle was dead. At seven and a half, she had lost her battle with leukemia. In a nursing home bed a few towns away, my mother lay in a coma. I thought the phone call might have been about her.

As I walked back through the tunnel, I thought about my career in medicine. I knew I would have to take night calls no matter what specialty I chose. I decided I would be willing to get up at night to deliver babies, to bring new life into the world. I would consider being an obstetrician and gynecologist.

DAY SIXTEEN

ROUGH WATERS

My fevers persist and the migraines are no better. Dr. Gregory visits again. His presence is welcome.

"The fevers are getting to me," I tell him.

He offers another explanation. "The fevers are your body fighting for you."

I appreciate the effort being made by my body to eliminate the germs, to fight for my life. My body is an ally! The migraine medicine will be adjusted and I'll see him in three days.

Taking my journal from the bedside table's top drawer, I write with my shaky hand, "So, Lord, I am thrilled to be alive at this time in my life. The challenges ahead don't thrill me. I am grateful not to know all that is ahead."

DAY EIGHTEEN

THE PIRATE

Since antibiotics and other measures have failed to diminish the high, spiking fevers, Drs. Brooks and Banks request a consultation by infectious disease (I.D.) specialists. Today a trio consisting of an I.D. fellow, a medical resident, and an intern come to evaluate me. The I.D. fellow interviews me, then asks me to sit up. Intense aching in my back and abdomen slow my sitting. The medical resident and intern watch as the fellow listens to my heart and lungs. "Your lungs are clear, the pneumonia seems to be gone," He says. He examines my nose, mouth, gums, throat, ears, and skin. He checks the lymph nodes in the front and back of my neck, under my jaw, over my collarbone, under my arms, inside my elbows, and in my groins. He presses on my abdomen and squeezes my calves. "We will discuss your case with the chief. He will be seeing you later today."

In the afternoon the chief enters, alone. He is a tall, thin, Caucasian man with a black left-eye patch. In a monotone he introduces himself as the Chief of Infectious Diseases. Then, speaking quite softly, he continues, "I have reviewed your case. I will now need to examine your testicles." Slowly I pull my johnny up and push the sheet down as he puts on gloves. He examines me and leaves.

What did he look for? What did he find? Why the eye patch? Why does he seem depressed? Ideas flurry past me. I hold on to one that brings me some amusement. I decide he is a depressed pirate.

That night, discussing the experience with my younger son, Dan, it all makes some sense. "The pirate wants one of my balls to fill his empty eye socket! Each is too large, and I have been spared!" We both laugh. "He would have more luck in pediatrics."

In the morning the pirate and his band return. They advise that an experimental antibiotic will be added to the four already being administered.

Anxiously, I await results. The fevers, up to 102.8, continue once or twice daily for three more days. Then temperature spikes gradually diminish to the 101s and 100s by week's end, on December twenty-fifth. A Christmas present.

DAY TWENTY-SIX

UNDAMAGED CHARTS

For the second time this week, Dr. Gregory sits with me. He asks, "How are you?"

"I feel so fragile and so loved at the same time," I tell him. I hesitate, then continue, "So much of my life is gone. I'm so limited as a husband. I'm not a partner or provider or best friend. I hope someday . . . I'll be a lover again." He waits for me to share more. "And, I do little for my friends and family. I receive a lot from my children and the larger family but give nothing to them. I'm too tired and too drugged to read." My eyes fill with hot tears.

Dr. Gregory offers, "This illness has not removed the wonderful times in your life."

Images race past my mind's eye: Summers as an adolescent working on a farm, studying at college, acceptance to medical school, receiving the Malcolm Pre-Medical Award, my mother attending my medical school graduation, joyous tears as I leave the church wed to Martha, making love, the births of my children, good friends, the men I call my "Dads"—Lloyd, Harvey, Rowe, and "Dad" Nicholson, my father-in-law—"as-good-as-it-gets" times with my office staff, the children's high school and college graduations, trips to Egypt and China, sailing, skiing, dancing, taking my first communion on Christmas Eve 1976, laughing at Carol Burnett, hearing Dizzy Gillespie in concert, performing in *The Gondoliers* and *The Boy Friend*, singing Christmas music in church, delivering babies, teaching at Johns Hopkins....

"I remember many wonderful times. Many moments of joy."

"Nothing can take those from you."

I look into Dr. Gregory's eyes. "I had a dream. It was Christmas at our home in New Hampshire. I unwrap a present—a cookbook for making candy. I follow the directions and before me is a tray of white glistening bunnies, with dark eyes, protruding upper center teeth, and pink inner ears pointing up. Then, I am upset to find that each rabbit has a tumor. I awoke feeling disgust."

Calmly, Dr. Gregory offers, "The candy may be the sweetness of life. It's been changed by the illness—the tumors." He smiles. He will see me again on Tuesday around eleven.

As he leaves, I think about my mother's life being changed by illness. At thirty-five she was given a diagnosis of Hodgkin's disease, cancer of the lymph system.

I remember back to a spring afternoon, when I was eleven. After walking home from school, I climbed up the back steps and opened the kitchen door. Mother sat at the table. I looked at her and stared at the bandages on her neck. Before I could ask, she said, "I had some tests today. I haven't been feeling well."

The following weekend she went away with her lifelong friend, Emma, to Pennsylvania. That Saturday, I made American-cheese sandwiches for lunch and my three-year-old brother Richard and I went out to eat them at the picnic table in the backyard. We heard the screen door slam and looked over to see our father slowly coming toward us. Wearing brown shorts, a faded tan short-sleeved shirt, and worn brown-leather sandals, his solid, muscular body seemed dejected as he walked with his shoulders forward and his head slightly bowed. Above his square face, wavy black hair was combed straight back, and below his furrowed brow his dull, gray-green eyes gazed sadly toward us. As he sat down at the far end of the table with his jaw clenched and his full lips tightly closed, his mouth quivered. "Your mother went with Emma to get some extra rest." Then he held his head in his hands and sobbed, "She has cancer." After a few sobs he continued, "I don't know what I will do. How can I raise you children?" Weeping, he stood and went back into the house.

"Why is Daddy crying?" Richard asked me.

"He's sad about Mommy being sick. Come and sit on my lap so I can hug you!" Richard's curly blond hair smelled sweet as I held him in my arms. I will protect and care for him, I thought.

That summer, mother had radiation treatments. She explained, "The doctor removed the cancer. The treatments are to be sure it won't come back. And we are not going to tell Grandma. It would upset her."

I don't know how or when my older brother Robert learned about her illness. And I do not remember all the specifics of her remissions and recurrences. But, in the spring of 1962, my sophomore year at college, she called from a hospital saying that she had some tests and was getting chemotherapy treatments. I offered to come home. "Stay at college and study," she urged. "I'm doing okay."

I hoped the chemotherapy would give her a long remission. I so wanted to become a doctor to help her be cured.

DAY TWENTY-EIGHT

GIFTS

Peach tones of morning sunlight color my bedspread on this new day. I smell the miniature spruce by the window and remember childhood Christmases and the excitement of unopened presents. Pushing the bed control buttons, I raise myself to a full sitting position. Turning to the bedside table, I study our family picture of a joyful moment last spring, when with radiant, smiling faces our healthy bodies embraced each other at Martha's fiftieth birthday celebration.

Opening the bedside table drawer, I retrieve my journal and write, "I have had a good Christmas. I felt the love of Martha, our children Bill, Dan and Heidi, our family, our church, and friends. I expressed my love for my family. No amount of pain will erase the memories of the best times of my life. I'll go with what I have, rather than wish I had more, or different. That was my life. Lord, You are a part of my strength every minute."

The weak, yellow-white sun is higher now and I remember that in the year prior to the surgery the prayers in my life had changed. What were once prayers of petition had become prayers of affirmation. From "God, be with me . . ." to "God, you are with me...."

I feel accepted by God.

Faith thrives when there is no hope but God.
—Ernest Gordon

DAYS THIRTY-TWO TO THIRTY-FIVE

CALM AND A STORM

I'm being discharged on New Year's Eve afternoon—I'm excited to be leaving in the same year I entered. With medications, IV fluids, instructions for a full liquid diet, supplies for redressing the drains, and Dr. Brooks' home phone number, Martha drives me the hour to her parent's home in Providence, Rhode Island.

Having aches rather than pains, no fevers over 100 for two days, and now tolerating liquids, I feel encouraged. I think the worst is behind me. I am going home to get well.

Making my way up the entry steps into the front hall, I breathe deeply, rapidly—huffing and puffing. After resting in a chair, I slowly climb the fourteen stairs to the second floor. Again winded, I start shaking as I enter the bedroom. Lying down, my teeth chatter and I shake uncontrollably. I feel so cold. My heart pounds so forcibly against my chest wall that my forest-green sweater moves with each beat. Is this a nervous response? I think so. I hope so. I won't let myself think it is anything else. Martha switches on the electric blanket and adds a quilt. The shaking chills diminish over ten minutes then stop. My temperature is 101.3. Exhausted, I fall asleep.

On New Year's Day I rest, and the nurse visits. I eat small amounts of custard and caramel yogurt, drink Ensure and cranberry juice, and take frequent naps. In late afternoon I feel cold, then colder, and begin shaking. Alarmed, I switch on the electric blanket and add more covers. I grit my teeth, tense the muscles in my face and abdomen, then my legs, arms, and chest to stop the shaking. The shivering and shaking overpower me. My temperature is 100.8. Martha consults with Dr. Brooks. She is instructed to call him any time the temperature is over 101.4 or my condition changes.

The next day I tolerate fluids, rice pudding, flan, and sorbet as well as a brief visit to the first floor. Then I nap.

Three hours later, I awake in late afternoon with energy. I feel stronger and encouraged. I take a shower with Martha's help. In the toasty bathroom the mirrors are steamed and I strip. She seals my left upper arm with plastic wrap to protect the PICC line. Under the water I soap my body and lather my hair. Rinsing the shampoo, I suddenly feel nauseated, weak, and lightheaded. The shivering begins. Then, the uncontrollable shaking. The chills may be from the stress of showering. Wrapped in towels, I lurch down the hall and collapse onto the bed. I hold my breath during the seizure-like spell.

"Breathe! Take a deep breath. Don't hold your breath!" Martha urges and demands. After this episode passes I lie limp and she takes my temperature—100.4. Is this another infection? I dread that possibility. I also dread another overpowering chill.

Martha is my Florence Nightingale. She changes the IV bags, gives medications, takes my temperature every six hours, and gives care and comfort. Dark rings surround her eyes and worry lines have deepened in her face. She smiles often and strokes my face and comforts me. "We'll get through this. We're a team," she says.

Uneasiness, headaches, and malaise accompany each fever. The shaking chills last many minutes. I am getting sicker. Martha takes my temperature and she calls Dr. Brooks. He advises that I be admitted early the next morning. I will undergo exploratory surgery to remove infected tissue and any other surgical procedures needed for healing. Both afraid and hopeful, I am also confused. Why am I worse? Is the perforation leaking? My spirit is spent. Will I make it through the night? Will I get there in time? What will be done? Will I recover?

I know that operating on me will be difficult for Dr. Brooks. Removing infected and scarred tissue from parts of the intestine and other abdominal organs requires delicate dissection of the unhealthy tissue from the viable. Many times I assisted general surgeons operating on patients with intra-abdominal infections from a perforated intestine or an infected, leaking gall bladder. The awful odor of infected tissues sometimes required a second mask or breathing through my mouth. And, infected tissues bleed easily and the bleeding can be difficult to stop. Dear God, be with me, and with Dr. Brooks. And guide his hands.

Under the portico at the hospital's main entrance the next morning I tremble as I lower myself into the wheelchair. In the admitting office I shiver violently while Martha answers questions and my blood is drawn. As I lie on a stretcher in the preop area of the operating room, waiting to be called, my weary mind wanders. Will I die during surgery? God, You are with me. Help me live.

Martha holds my hand and we have this precious time together. After a tender kiss, I am taken into an operating room for the second operation. I want to live and be well again.

DAYS THIRTY-FIVE TO THIRTY-SEVEN

ADRIFT

I awake. I see my room. I survived the surgery. Groggy and exhausted, the hours pass. Friends and family come and go. Is it day or night? Am I dreaming? I'm not sure of much.

I feel my abdomen. I have a long bandage in the middle and a tube coming out midway on the left. I think it's the second day after surgery. I ask Martha, "What did Dr. Brooks do?" She takes my hand.

"He removed infected tissue."

"Did he close the perforation?"

"He couldn't because of the infection."

"What else?"

"Part of your pancreas was removed."

"Oh. That's why the nurses prick a finger every few hours—to test blood sugar and see if I'm developing diabetes. What's the tube?"

"It goes into your Jay . . .," she hesitates.

"Jejunum, the second part of the small intestine."

"It's a J-tube for putting nutrition in the intestine."

"I thought he would close the perforation," I say. "Removing part of the pancreas, I may become diabetic." Then I ask myself questions I can't answer. Will I digest food someday? Will I get pancreatitis again? Will I make it? Will I ever be healthy again?

DAY FORTY

A MOUTHFUL

Something on my tongue surprises me as I awaken. Sticking my tongue out, then retracting it against my upper front teeth, I scrape an odorless, tasteless, thick, soft-yet-textured material onto my upper teeth. I brushed my teeth last night, so what can it be?

Rolling onto my left side, then rising slowly, I make my way to the sink and look in the mirror. I see white clumps on my teeth, gums, tongue, throat, and roof of my mouth. Gagging, I fight back a wave of nausea and break into a cold sweat.

"Oh, how disgusting! I have thrush. I have fungus growing in my mouth and throat! Gross! I am DEBILITATED!"

Being debilitated scares me. Is this the beginning of the end? Am I immunosuppressed? Did I contract AIDS from one of my many blood transfusions? Or is this just the consequence of so many antibiotics for so long? In my years as a physician, I never had a patient this sick.

The operations and the anemia of chronic illness have resulted in eleven blood transfusions. I must have a third operation to put my intestines back together so I can eat. Will I survive an operation in this weakened state? How can I get stronger before surgery? Will I get hepatitis? Will I have the J-tube in forever? Or, will I always get tube feedings and TPN?

I pray, "O God, You accompany me in all my efforts."

Later in the morning, I swizzle a bitter, mint-flavored antifungal solution. I brush my tongue, teeth, and gums often. I check my mouth each time I pass the mirror that day. No immediate improvement. I wonder how long I will have this infection.

DAY FORTY-THREE

LIGHTS IN THE DARKNESS

Alone, I lie on my back watching sheets of rain drive against the windows. Dark clouds whip across the mottled gray sky. With low hope for my future, I wonder if the perforation will ever heal and if I will ever be well again.

Feeling lonely, I reach into my pale-blue pajama shirt pocket and slowly take out a folded card. Carefully, I open the buff-colored card with royal-blue edges. Martha gave it to me five days ago, before she went to the Caribbean for a few days with her family. Now again I read:

"A—You are my darling.
You have loved me so fully for the last twenty years that I am truly a different person—changed by your love.

My darling—
My soulmate—how lucky and blessed we are to have found each other in this lifetime and in this world.
I love you with all my heart—M"

As I feel her love, warm tears fill my eyes to the brim. Calmly, I close them and a few drops streak across my cheeks. She calls daily from Antigua and we talk. Sometimes I fight back a lump in my throat that could start me weeping. I worry that Martha may not come back. What if her plane crashes? I know she needs a break from this awful odyssey. I'm not getting worse, or better. With her away, I am often lonely and repeatedly read her card during these days and nights. Tomorrow she returns, I hope.

On this dark day, I decide to call Lloyd, one of the men I think of as my "Dads." While Adam Lohaus fathered me, by age ten we were estranged. Unknowingly, I then sought refuge from him and pieced together a whole "Dad" from friendships with three other men: Lloyd, Rowe, and Harvey.

LLOYD

Lloyd now lives in Philadelphia and we have spoken during these weeks in the hospital in Boston. I met him when needing a counselor for the Boy Scout's God and Country Award. He supported that interest and became a friend in 1959, when my parents divorced. Lloyd and his wife Eliza became extended family, visiting me during the summers and inviting me to visit them during my college years and beyond. He shared his love of life and birds of prey. Starting in September 1976, I joined him at Hawk Mountain, Pennsylvania, to experience the raptor migration and on many trips to observe eagles.

I sought time with him after his own serious health setback in 1998. We traveled to Vera Cruz, Mexico, with a "birding group" to watch the raptors' winter arrival into Central America. Comfortable as roommates, we talked easily about our life journeys and our friendship. On one occasion I told him, "I valued your support and never asked you for money for my education."

"I know you didn't," he said, "but I would have given it to you." Somehow I knew he would support me in any way I would ask. His interest in my life came with encouragement and optimism and without judgment or advice. That is why I want to talk to him now. Dialing his number, I wait while the phone rings.

"Hello," Lloyd answers.

"Lloyd, this is Allan."

"How are you?" he asks kindly.

"I'm pretty sick . . . I need to see you."

"I know it hasn't been going well. I am quite concerned . . . I'll visit you in the next few days, as soon as I can."

"Thanks, Lloyd. See you soon.... Bye."

Two days later he sits at my Boston bedside. As I study his blue eyes, bushy white eyebrows, and broad easy smile, I think, *I may be seeing him for the last time.*

He holds my hand with his, strong and freckled. I feel the warmth of our friendship. "You'll make it," he says. "Keep fighting . . . You'll be healthy again."

"I will."

ROWE

When I was almost eleven, I went to a Boy Scout troop meeting held in the gym of our town's junior high school. I met the Scoutmaster, Ford, a tall soldier-like man, and his assistant, Rowe, a wiry man with a toothy smile and large, kind eyes. I met boys of many different backgrounds and faiths. Some had funny nicknames like Pochi, Jigger, Cheezy, Dondi, and Skeeter. Being chubby I became "Crisco"— fat in the can. Then, that September, when Ford retired, Rowe became our Scoutmaster.

As I write this memoir, I look often at Rowe's picture on my desk and think about his guidance on my journey to manhood and beyond.

In scouting, fulfilling specific requirements has rewards. After learning the Scout oath, motto, handshake, certain knots, and completing a hike I received my Tenderfoot badge. Rowe encouraged me to become a Second Class Scout, then First Class and, over the next five years, Star, Life, and, finally, Eagle Scout.

Breaking rules in scouting had consequences. One morning at summer camp in the Adirondacks, I sat on my bunk and looked out. Seeing no one stirring, I lit a match and puffed a cigarette, not knowing how to inhale.

"Lohaus! What are you doing?" Rowe yelled in a voice of the World War II infantryman he had been. "Come over here!" he ordered from his tent across the clearing.

"I don't have shoes on."

"Put on your rubbers! And bring those cigarettes!"

Standing in front of his tent, I trembled. He extended his hand. I surrendered the pack of Old Gold's. He looked me in the eye. "There is no smoking allowed at Camp Read."

"I know that, Rowe," I whispered fearfully.

"Go and clean the latrine. I'll inspect it in thirty minutes."

As I approached the four-holer, I knew I would never smoke at camp again.

Our scout troop disbanded in 1987. But in August, 2001, some of Rowe's "boys" gathered to celebrate him at an afternoon picnic. The smells of wood smoke and roasting hot dogs took us back to campfires of the 1950s. Stories of our lives with him filled the time together; we honored this ninety-one-year-old self-taught horticulturist with only an eighth grade education who was a "Dad" to many of us.

As shadows crept over the picnic, I prepared to leave. I embraced him and kissed his right cheek, then his left, as he kissed mine.

"Take care of yourself, Kid," he said gently.

"I will," I whispered. "You take care, too."

HARVEY

I'd like to work on a farm," I told my mother when I was almost fourteen. She suggested I write to family friends living on a farm and ask them if they, or someone they knew, needed a boy for the summer. A reply came from their friends, Helen and Harvey, a middle-aged sister and brother with a dairy farm called Willowbrook Farm in Clinton Corners, New York, about fifty miles to the north of White Plains. Harvey had a boy help him each summer and needed one for this summer, 1957.

On a Saturday, Mother and I drove to Willowbrook Farm and talked with Helen and Harvey in the parlor of their large two-story, chocolate-ice-cream-brown shingled house. I liked Harvey's calm, friendly face. We then looked at the spacious first-floor corner room overlooking the brook, which would be "my room." They offered me a job.

When school ended, I packed my things, including jeans, new work boots, blue denim shirts, and three red bandanas. My parents drove me to the farm the next Saturday.

Harvey came from the house to greet us wearing a gray-and-white-striped cap, like a train engineer, and matching bib overalls over a blue denim shirt. He smiled as we stepped from our station wagon to greet him.

"Hello," he said as Helen came from the house. I shook his hand and stood next to him. Being five feet, ten inches, I was slightly taller than he was and, at 200 pounds, a lot heavier. His overalls fit easily over his trim body. His strong, suntanned arms and hands hung comfortably from his faded shirtsleeves. He wore a hearing aid.

After lunch, my parents left. I unpacked, then put on my farm clothes. That June afternoon my apprenticeship began as Harvey taught me some of the evening chores: bringing the cows in from the pasture to the barnyard, assembling the milking machines, and carrying pails of warm sweet-smelling milk to the refrigerated tank and pouring it through the filter without spilling a drop. After milking, we let the herd out to the evening pasture and collected eggs in the chicken coop. We took grain to the calves in the paddock and then went to the house for supper.

That summer, Harvey patiently and gently taught me the skills of driving a tractor, spreading manure, and loading hay wagons. I also learned that safety came first. Always. He asked me to do what he knew I could, including climbing to the top of the thirty-five-foot silo to secure the pipe used to fill it with chopped green corn.

Reaching the top of the silo, I stood on a small platform and waited for the pipe to be raised. I heard distant thunder. Tense and scared, I looked at the lightning rod on the silo's very top. Would it work or would I be electrocuted? A cool breeze blew toward the growing thunderheads. I secured the fill pipe quickly as thunder rolled around me. "Come down, Allan, we're finished," Harvey finally called. With my legs shaking, I climbed down each narrow metal rung, holding my breath. I jumped from the last step as raindrops hit my back and arms. During the summers on the farm, I would build on this experience in self-discipline and courage.

Years later, I understood more fully what else began that June afternoon at Willowbrook Farm. I had found a refuge from my father's criticism and my parents' conflicts. With Harvey's gentleness for all living things, I felt safe. With him I felt accepted. A man of few words, he often answered my "what if" questions with, "We'll cross that bridge when we come to it."

On the farm, I experienced the forces and rhythms of nature and the beauty of new life. And I learned not to cry over spilled milk, or cracked eggs—we ate them scrambled.

Harvey and I rarely touched physically. Sometimes we bumped while working in tight places or our hands touched when passing a tool or bucket. Yet, twice during each of the five summers we worked together, we touched by intention—we shook hands on the day I arrived and the day I left. When Harvey died at eighty-six, Helen held onto my arm as we entered the Poughkeepsie Friends Meeting House for his memorial service and again at his burial.

I was honored to be a man who had come of age in their family.

DAY FIFTY

A VESSEL

A s the sun approaches Boston's western skyline, I lie alone in bed and hold a statuette of Our Lady of Lourdes in my right hand. Cast in white, her habit's blue folds part around prayerfully clasped hands. She wears a blue crown and her peaceful face turns slightly to the right and downward. She contains holy water. I have held her an hour since Martha's mother visited and gave her to me. The Lady is a gift for my healing from my mother-in-law's hairdresser, Susan. Four years ago, Susan went to Lourdes after her second mastectomy and brought back two statuettes. She used one for herself. Knowing of my operations and prolonged recovery, she sent this one to me. I hope this holy gift from France will cure me. I doubt that it can. Yet, I am eager to use it.

I wondered what I should do. Apply the water to my abdominal incisions? To my painful back and right flank? To the healing drain sites? Can I sip it? I loosen the crown and bring the open vessel closer for a whiff. It has a faint, familiar aroma . . . of plastic.

I need to know how to use it. My best friend from boyhood, Dondi, who is a priest, can give me answers. I dial the phone.

"St. Columbo's," a youthful voice answers.

"This is Doctor Allan Lohaus calling Monsignor Lagonegro."

"He is not available. Would you like to leave a message?"

"Yes. Please ask him to return a call to me at Brigham Hospital in Boston. Thank you."

Placing the Lady on the bedside table to my right, I remember a warm spring Friday evening in 1957, when Dondi and I were fourteen. Walking home from a Silver Lake Boy Scout troop meeting, we stopped under a street lamp. A gentle warm breeze touched us and the trees nearby. He spoke in a calm and earnest voice, "I've been thinking a lot about what I'm going to do. What I want to become." After a long pause he continued, "I want to become a priest."

"I think you should do what you really want to do," I told him. Then, I asked, "Where will you go?"

"I'll go to seminary in New York City, if my parents let me."

"When will you start?"

"Next fall."

"Then we won't be together anymore?"

"No. But we can stay friends."

Walking home alone from the corner, I already missed my best friend.

In April 1969 Father Dominik Lagonegro celebrated his first mass at St. Anthony's Catholic Church in Silver Lake. I came from my internship in New Jersey to attend. Both our careers began that summer.

The ringing phone brings me back to Boston.

"Allan?"

"Yes."

"This is Dondi. How are you?"

"Pretty darn good."

"I pray for you each day."

"I'm glad you do. And thanks for calling back—it's so good to hear your voice. I called because I've been given some holy water from Lourdes and I'm wondering what people do with it."

"You can rub it on your skin or any sore places."

"What about scars?"

"That would be fine."

"Can I drink it?"

"I've never heard of anyone doing that!" Dondi exclaimed with amusement.

"Thanks, Dondi"

"God bless you."

With excitement I rub drops of holy water onto seven scars. I go to the mirror and check my mouth, gums, and tongue. The thrush is gone, so I won't rinse my mouth with holy water.

The cityscape twinkles. I have hope.

DAY FIFTY-FIVE

BELLS

Ding-ding-dong! Ding-ding-dong! Ding-ding-dong! The triple-beep alarm of the pump delivering intravenous medication beeps constantly, minute after minute. I pushed the nurse-call button awhile ago, when the alarm started. A nurses' aide appeared promptly, understood the problem, and said that she would tell the nurse.

Ding-ding-dong! Ding-ding-dong! The bells drone on. Can I stop the alarm? Dare I push the nurse-call button again? Can I switch the IV bags? Turn off the pump? Cover my head with a pillow? Alone and needing help, will anyone come? An aide? A nurse? Martha? A visitor? Anyone?

Too weak to stand and push the poles and pumps into the hall to the nurses' station, I can only lay back and close my eyes. I hear the tune, *Ding-ding-dong, ding-ding-dong.* Dot-dot-dash, dot-dot-dash. Up your ass, up your ass. *Damn! Merde! Shit! What can I do?*

The only thing I can do is have a different attitude. The choice is mine. *Ding-ding-dong, ding-ding-dong.* Now, new words come to me for the tune.

Ding-ding-dong, ding-ding-dong. God is here, God is near. God is here, God is near.

Calmly I repeat this as the bells ring on and on.

DAY FIFTY-NINE

MENUS

W hat are you having for dinner tonight?" Martha asks.

"Tonight is roasted, smoked turkey breast with cranberry chutney, wild rice, and green beans with almonds," I reply with playful enthusiasm. Each "entrée" I receive arrives punctually at four-thirty in the afternoon when a nurse brings the day's third bag of Total Parenteral Nutrition (TPN), which is a quart and a half of chilled, white liquid administered through the PICC line. I have been allowed no solid food by mouth since the day the general surgeon told me the "bad news" that I had a duodenal perforation requiring weeks to heal, maybe longer.

On that "bad-news" day, fifty-nine days ago, my friend Mike was with me, helping with my care and giving support. I told him I wanted to make a list of my favorite foods that I would eat when the perforation healed. Taking a yellow notebook from his shirt pocket, our eyes met and he began writing. When finished, the list we titled *Allan's Food List* had recorded a total of eighty-nine drinks, appetizers, entrées, deserts, snacks, and special meals that included asparagus rolled in ham with cream cheese, Austrian wursts in split green-pea soup, blueberry buttermilk pancakes, Virgin Piña coladas, watermelon that was lightly salted, and yellow ribbon candy (See Appendix).

And let me not overlook the treat I enjoy on afternoon walks through the medical and surgical unit—fresh, fragrant buttered popcorn that comes out from under the nurses' lounge door between two-thirty and three o'clock. I can taste it, I just can't see it or chew it. My heightened sense of smell makes it a five-star quick fix and I imagine it to be Newman's Own, my favorite.

Tomorrow for dinner I'll have a petite filet, or perhaps roast duck. I'm undecided.

DAY SIXTY-FOUR

GUARDIAN ANGEL

As I lie on my back, hot tears well up in my eyes, skating across my cheeks and into my beard and ears. Dr. Gregory sits with me and listens. After a long pause, I begin in a trembling whisper, "Martha has been with me each day for all these months." Droplets flow and I feel gratitude for all my wife has done, for all she is doing. "She calls at night to check with the nurses." My quiet weeping blurs the room. "She washes my hair and trims my beard." Trickling tears warm my cool face. "She has a mission to get me home alive." I begin to sob. The sobbing ends when I take a few deep breaths.

I turn and look at Dr. Gregory. His gray-blue eyes are deep, concerned, friendly, and peaceful. He smiles knowingly. I continue, "When the chaplain stopped in last night, I asked her to read the Twenty-third Psalm. I think I am in the Valley of the Shadow of Death . . . my tears are the comforting still waters." He nods knowingly.

We sit in silence and I let the tears dry on my face. I feel comforted and stronger.

After the session with Dr. Gregory, Martha senses my hope. "We need a calendar," she announces brightly.

"I like that idea. We can hang it up next to the sink. I'd like to put on Dan's May graduation day at the School of Visual Arts in New York City. I really want to go to it with you."

"That's three months away," she encourages.

"Either my perforation will heal or I must be operated on again. I really hope I'll be able to go."

Dan visits me in Boston every two weeks while completing his senior thesis, a documentary film titled *Traffic Jam* that he is writing, directing, producing, and editing. He is graduating on what I jokingly call the "Ten-Year College Plan," he started in 1989 and will finish this year in 1999. "I really want to see his film and meet his adviser and friends," I tell my wife. "I want to cheer when he crosses the stage with his diploma. I want to be there."

I think about our other grown children, Heidi in Los Angeles and Bill near San Francisco who haven't been east since Christmas. I miss them.

When I awake from a nap Martha presents me with a 1999 calendar containing nature photos. She hangs it and writes in Dan's graduation and our birthdays.

We claim our future.

DAY SIXTY-FIVE

LIFEBOAT

Anxiety floods over my exhausted spirit. Yet, I still have the desire and faith to pray. I sing a childhood prayer song from Quaker First Day School: "Lord who lovest little children/I lift my heart in prayer to Thee." After singing it twice, I hum it, then I pray, "God, You are with me in all my efforts. With me to sit up. To stand. To walk. To see the face of Jesus in the caregivers. To guide the hands of those doing procedures on my body. To thank those who support me. To appreciate those who comfort me. To sense the Holy Spirit being with me as I experience this mysterious illness."

Messages from all parts of America and beyond bring the love and prayers of family and friends. In San Diego and Providence, Rhode Island, as well as in New Hampshire and Maryland, churches know of me and pray for my recovery. Prayer chains connect me to hundreds of hearts and souls. Often when I go to the sink I read Jeremiah's words on a card tacked there: "The Lord will bring healing and health, and hope for your future."

Last evening as Dan ended his visit, he came to my bedside. Robust at twenty-eight years and standing six feet four inches, he leaned over me and slid his hands and arms under my back and around my shoulders. He pressed his warm, stubbly face against mine and spoke softly into my right ear, "Stay strong, Pop. I love you."

Now I lie alone. A husband and father too weak to stand without help. A clinician and teacher too weary to think or read. Illness has set me adrift from my life. But I know with certainty that I am loved and accepted by God. I have accepted that I am accepted. Only the spiritual grounds me. Filled with peace, I am carried in a lifeboat that is love.

DAY SIXTY-EIGHT

ANOTHER VESSEL

L ying in bed on a Sunday afternoon, a gentle knock brings an unexpected visit from New Hampshire neighbors—John, a retired minister and his wife Elaine.

"We detoured here to see you on our way home from Cape Cod."

They inspect the room, Martha, and me. After pleasantries and a weather report from our home on Trask Mountain, Elaine says, "We would like to pray with you."

"That's fine, I like prayers."

I look up at them standing at my bedside. She extends both hands and takes my right hand in hers. John takes a brass bottle from his pocket and says, "I have this oil with me."

I close my eyes.

As if in a pulpit, he preaches, "I want you to know that Jesus loves you." As he prays aloud, his oiled finger makes a cross on my forehead, " . . . in the name of Jesus Christ, our Lord."

I've been anointed! I'm shocked! Has he given me Last Rites? Does he *know* I need this? Am I going to be dead soon? Does he know or care what relationship I have with God or with Jesus?

The prayer being finished, I open my eyes. They smile, embrace Martha, and leave, shutting the door behind them. I turn toward my wife, "Wow, I can't believe that."

"I can't either," she says.

"I remember reading that religion is for those who fear Hell; spirituality is for those who have been there." I rub the oil into my forehead. It can't hurt. My skin is so dry.

During the first weeks of this illness I spoke with a med-school buddy, Steve, now a psychiatrist in California.. He told me, "Studies show patients who are prayed for have better outcomes than those not prayed for, whether the patients know they are prayed for or not. I am praying for you."

As a surgeon, I encouraged patients at their preoperative consultation to have their clergy visit them in the hospital. And clergy sometimes attended the preoperative consultations as well. I was comfortable with both. As a surgeon I carefully put the tissues together, and, while I know the physiology of wound healing, I believe that spiritual energy helps the tissues heal and prayer may direct that energy.

DAY SIXTY-NINE

COURSE CHANGE

Rufus, a husky Jamaican transportation aide, enters my room. Wearing scrubs and thick gold necklaces, rings, and bracelets, his familiar smile includes gold teeth. "Ready for X-ray?"

"Yes, I'm ready. Can I go by stretcher?"

"I have a wheelchair . . . but sure, I'll get one."

Going for my eighth CT scan, I want comfort and warmth as sometimes the wait in radiology is cold, lasting forty minutes or more. I simply can't sit up that long. Today's CT will determine if the perforation has closed and I can eat.

Slowly climbing onto the stretcher, I lower my back onto the elevated headrest and Rufus tucks a blanket around me. As he pulls up the side rails I ask, "Rufus, can you do me a small favor?"

"Sure."

"Do we have time for a short stop on the way to X-ray?"

"Sure, where?"

I look him right in the eye, "The Viagra Clinic."

With a burst of laughter, he says, "I want to try that stuff myself."

The CT results disappoint me; the perforation has not healed. Liquids from my intestine are continuing to leak into my abdominal cavity. Drs. Brooks and Banks confer and recommend another month for healing. If the intestine has not healed by then, surgery must be performed.

I will be sent to a skilled nursing facility to continue tube feedings and intravenous nutrition and to start physical therapy. I have to walk again and gain strength. I want a room with a different view.

DAY SEVENTY-ONE

NAVIGATING

L eaving Boston by ambulance, I am going to Beechwood, a skilled nursing and rehabilitation facility in Providence, Rhode Island. Martha will live with her parents a few blocks away.

On this bright, blue-sky morning, Martha helps me dress, then packs the flowers, CD player, toiletries, clothes, our family picture, and my journal. She hand-carries an envelope with medical records and the care protocols for the J-tube and PICC line.

The ambulance staff, who look like Mutt and Jeff, help me onto their stretcher. With goodbyes to the head nurse, Julie, and the staff, I'm taken down the elevator and out through the ambulance entrance near the emergency room. In the ambulance I ride backwards looking out the windows to my left and through the rear doors. Almost instantly, I notice our route is northeast. Rhode Island is south. I wonder why.

"How are you going to Providence?" I ask the driver.

"Storrow Drive to I-93, then south on I-95."

That route will add half an hour to the trip. Yet, I feel no urgency. I am comfortable, and not wearing an adult diaper. My last bowel movement was just after the second surgery five weeks ago. Passing the fuel storage tank in South Boston painted with a colorful Sister Corita Kent design, we now travel south. I begin to feel cold.

"Could I have another blanket and some heat?" I ask.

"Shuah." Jeff answers in his South Boston accent, then climbs back and covers me; the heater fan begins to hum.

"Do you know Blackstone Boulevard?"

Mutt replies, "Nevah been ta Providence. Da office gave us dees directions."

"How are we getting there?"

"It says to take I-95 to exit one."

"Really? My in-laws live near there and when we drive to their place we get off at exit twenty-seven . . . . I think exit one is in the southern part of Rhode Island near the Connecticut State line. Exit one is for Westerly, not Providence. Can you call your office?"

"Dis is what day gave us."

Stretching anxiously, I look back over my left shoulder to see signs in the northbound lanes.

"We just passed exit twenty-seven," I tell them. "Get off at the next exit and go north one exit." They take my advice and slowing, we exit, reverse direction, and approach exit twenty-seven from the south.

"Stay to the right as you exit. Bear left at the first fork."

I see the familiar railroad-car diner that confirms we're now on the right route; Mutt is following my directions and he asks, "How do we go now?"

"Bear right at the next fork. As you come down a long hill you will see stores and a gas station on the right. At that traffic light turn left onto Blackstone Boulevard. In about a half mile, Beechwood will be on the left."

"Really?"

"Trust me, I was a Boy Scout."

Within a few minutes I hear him exclaim, "Hey, there it is!"

Will they make it back to Boston, I wonder?

DAY SEVENTY-FIVE

PRESIDENT'S DAY

Today, the second Monday in February of 1999, I will again be transfused with blood. Being so ill for so long, my bone marrow is producing little new blood. My weak and weary muscles tremble sometimes at rest and frequently with minimal activity. My blood count is less than half that of a healthy person. Any bleeding could quickly become a life-ending crisis. At nine o'clock in the morning I am transported by wheelchair in a van to a nearby hospital.

After an hour in the ER waiting room my back aches intensely from sitting. I ask the clerk where I may lie down. I am told there are no beds or stretchers available, but that I will be called soon. During the next hour the TV blares Jerry Springer and his guests, exposing the angry, relationship-challenged, sexually explicit victims and persecutors. One hour of this is one too many.

After three hours of waiting, I am called to be seen in an inner ER waiting room. There are chairs, but no stretchers. A doctor reviews my history and admits me. Patients are transfused in the outpatient hematology center except on holidays. Today I'll be admitted to the third-floor medical unit.

Fatigue numbs me. I overhear the clerk report that the room is ready and transport is on the way. After twenty minutes I ask the staff to check on transport. I close my eyes, listen to my breathing, and count the minutes, one for every fifteen breaths. The "driver" appears and pushes me in the wheelchair down the halls, around the corners, over bumps, and into an elevator.

At the third-floor desk the nurse directs the driver to take me to Room 375, Bed B. We reach the room and pass Bed A, where a frail woman sits with a very thin elderly patient who barely makes wrinkles under the sheets. On the other side of the curtain I lie down, exhausted. Martha sits in a chair. I am glad for her commitment and love. By this time I expected we would be back at Beechwood. A hellish day so far.

The nurse comes in and asks Martha, "Are you Ellen Lohaus?"

"No," Martha replies and points at me. "He is *Allan*."

A quick glance at me and the nurse's voice becomes high-pitched, "He can't be in here. It's illegal! This is a female room!"

It is a Presidents' Day Special! Transfusions and a gender change both for one low price!

Moved to Room 373, I lie on a lumpy bed, probably used in World War II, with two pillows that feel like Idaho potatoes. What a day.

At four P.M. the first unit of blood is running; two units will follow, finishing between one and three in the morning. I will be spending the night. While the second unit is running, I struggle to sit, then stand and push both IV poles to the room's far corner to get my parka. Back to bed with it, the uncomfortable pillows go, and the rolled parka becomes a pillow. This is rough.

I think of Chris, a physician friend, who is now in his seventies. At age sixteen he was imprisoned by the Japanese in a POW camp in Indonesia. Clothed in rags, starved and beaten, he had years of hell. Yet he survived with dignity and a joyful spirit. He did it—I can too.

If I let myself be consumed by hate I would be squandering the life that has been given back to me.

—Ernest Gordon

DAYS SEVENTY-SIX TO EIGHTY-FIVE

PROGRESS

During these ten days at the skilled nursing facility my strength and walking improve. I learn to walk without the support of the IV pole and I progress from climbing three stairs to eleven—an entire flight! One day the physical therapist takes me outside to walk on a path. The sun warms my face. I feel stronger. Then, she surprises me.

"Let's walk backward."

"I'll try." Placing my right foot back, then my left, it feels like the first time I have ever done this. I stagger and she steadies me, supporting my arm.

"Good. Keep on going."

We walk backward on a path for a while then forward across an uneven lawn.

I am making progress. The next day, after my nap, my father-in-law, "Dad" Nicholson, visits and we play pool in the patient lounge. It is a fun day.

On the morning of the eighty-fifth day, Martha drives me to our New Hampshire home.

DAY EIGHTY-SIX

AN ISLAND

Sitting at home in a recliner, I am bathed in sunlight shining through a living-room skylight. On this clear winter day I look north fifty-five miles and see Mt. Washington and other snow-capped presidentials. At last Martha and I have privacy and a life together. Yet, I worry about being so far from Boston. Could I get there in time with an emergency? A high fever? Internal bleeding? What if I need hospitalization? I won't go to the local hospital where this all started. I must get to Boston somehow. My weekly appointments in town with Dr. Bowen, the gastroenterologist, help me to be physically stable. He adjusts the IV and TPN feedings, stopping my weight loss and then reversing it. He manages episodes of dehydration with IV fluids at home and, at today's visit, offered an unusual treatment for my problem of intense thirst.

"Sometimes I am so thirsty I feel desperate. What can I do?"

"Get a small pebble and suck on it."

"Are you kidding?"

"No, it will stimulate your saliva without triggering digestive enzymes as hard candy would do."

"I'll try it."

Once home I find a smooth white stone the size of my smallest fingernail in a potted plant. I wash it, boil it in the microwave, and place it on my tongue. When I suck the pebble, I salivate and can swallow, being careful to keep the pebble between my lower lip and gum. I store the pebble in my shirt pocket when not using it. While I am glad to have relief of my constant thirst, I wonder when I will drink and eat normally again.

During this time at home Martha gives almost all my nursing care. She takes my temperature, prepares the IV, TPN feedings, and J-tube feedings, mixes medications, and administers them all. She makes my bed, helps me shower, changes my bandages, empties the urinal, and evacuates the suction bulb attached to the drain placed near my right kidney. The bulb collects putrid-smelling drainage. We both breathe through our mouths during this procedure. Beyond the help that Martha gives me, a visiting nurse comes twice a week, takes my blood pressure and pulse, and changes the sterile PICC-line dressing.

Martha, my visiting nurse, and the PICC line are my lifeline at home. Without them I would still be in the skilled nursing facility. While I improved greatly while at Beechwood, I particularly do not miss the facility's dietary aides knocking on my door in the afternoon, waking me and asking, "Would you like a snack?"

"No, I don't eat anything," I said each time they asked.

And on some evenings, between seven-thirty and eight o'clock, a different aide would knock, waking me again, and ask, "Can I take your supper tray?"

"No thanks, I didn't have one today."

Life is good in this refuge.

DAY NINETY-ONE

SIGHTINGS

In midmorning, I awake in bed in my first-floor den. The IV pole stands next to me, the empty urinal bottle leans against it. The IV pump and charger sit on the bedside table next to a silver bell Christmas ornament that I ring when I need Martha. On the far wall, a contemporary teak bureau top holds medicine bottles, peroxide, gauze pads, sterile wipes, and syringes. Above them hangs a pastel of Wonder Lake and the Alaska Range in autumn. The sliding glass doors to my left face south and the sun beams through. Lying in bed and looking out I notice movement on the snow. An arctic hare, pure white, bounds from left to right through the trees and shrubs. Its fluid motion takes me beyond the window vista. Moments later, a German shepherd moves haltingly along the hare's trail, sniffing the tracks. He'll never catch the hare. I am glad.

When I get up, I move slowly to shower. In the warm bathroom looking at myself in the mirror, I take off my dark-blue flannel robe and glance first at the J-tube anchored in my mid-abdomen and then at the drains and scars. Quickly, I look away. I'm not ready to face this. Martha wraps my left upper arm in a tea towel then in plastic wrap to keep the PICC line dry. I balance with my hands on the walls and my feet widely apart. Then, taking small steps, I go into the stall and under the warm water. I lather my right hand and wash my body with it. In moments I'm shivering, then shaking. My teeth chatter. I must get out. No shampoo today.

Wrapped in towels, I lie under a comforter. Martha lies with me and shares her warmth, holding my face in her hands. "Are you okay?"

"I can't stop shaking." As I look into her eyes, I wonder, *Is this my last shower? Am I dying? Do I have an infection in my blood stream? Severe anemia?*

"I'll ask Dr. Bowen to check my blood count," I stammer.

"You'll see him tomorrow. But the visiting nurse comes this afternoon. Maybe she can draw the blood so he'll have it tomorrow."

"That's a good idea. Will you call his office to order it?" When the shivering stops, Martha calls.

Too tired to move, I sleep in our bedroom.

DAY ONE HUNDRED TWELVE

TORPEDOES

O h! Ouch! Ooooh!" I gasp as sharp pains in my abdomen and pelvis start during this evening's J-tube feeding. They ease momentarily; then, stabbing pains near the tube site and intense aching deeper toward my bladder force me to hold my breath, tense my abdomen, and grimace. "Oh . . .," I groan. "Oh, it hurts. I can't take this."

"Martha," I shout. "Martha, can you hear me?" She may not hear my weakened voice. Oh, this is bad. "Muff, I need you!" I groan.

She runs into the room asking, "What is it? How can I help you?"

"I'm having awful cramps. Turn off the J-tube pump and call Dr. Brooks."

"I'm so sorry," she says and turns off the pump, strokes my forehead, and reaches for the phone. Dr. Brooks advises discontinuing the tube feedings and using Tylenol rectal suppositories for the pains. He asks to be called during the night if the pains worsen and in the morning for an update.

Putting on a glove, I expertly insert the medicine. Waiting for relief, I rest and reflect that, for me, this past December could have been called "Rectal Suppository Month" since, with so many high fevers, I needed many suppositories and learned quickly to administer my own. Today, as I perform this delicate procedure, I imagined filming an outrageous patient education video.

Speaking to the audience in my video I advise, "Glove your dominant hand and spread your knees. With your nondominant hand gently grasp your scrotum, if you have one, and pull it upward. Dip the gloved index finger in lubricant and apply it on the anus and into the opening. Firmly grip the suppository with the pointed end toward you and slowly place it deep in the rectum beyond the sphincter, so it won't pop out. Release scrotum if necessary, and remove the glove."

The background music rises and the credits roll. But what music? Beethoven? Vivaldi? No, Mozart. He was bawdy.

In the morning, Martha drives us to Boston for my fifth hospital admission.

DAY ONE HUNDRED NINETEEN

GUIDANCE

We will be holding you in prayer the night before your surgery," my friends Dave and Barbara tell me by phone. "We have invited many from your church to our home at seven o'clock."

That evening, when thirty gathered at Dave and Barbara's house in Maryland, Martha and I have our own prayer time in my hospital room on Boston's Francis Street. We pray silently, then aloud. We sense a divine presence with us. Our eyes meet.

"They are praying for us in Columbia, I feel it," I say to her.

"So do I."

"We are so lucky to have their support."

"Can you imagine going through this without them?" Martha says. "Without all our family and friends? Without all the support we have?"

She climbs into bed with me. We lie cheek to cheek and share a long embrace. We have strength for tomorrow's operation. I fall asleep in her arms.

At eleven o'clock that evening, Marie, an attractive Jamaican aide, takes my vitals—blood pressure, pulse, respirations, and temperature. As her dark eyes meet mine, she smiles and says, "Doctor, I pray for you each night."

"Thank you, Marie."

"Tonight I will pray that your operation goes well."
My eyes fill with tears. "Thank you, Marie," I whisper.
"I'll see you tomorrow evenin'."

DAY ONE HUNDRED TWENTY

MOONLESS NIGHT

A wakening in darkness, I see a shadowy figure, maybe Martha? Groggy and sedated, I ask, "Where am I?"

"In your room." It's her voice. She touches my forehead.

"Was I in Recovery Room?"

"Yes, three hours."

"What happened?"

"A lot."

"Is that blood running?"

"Yes, your fourth unit since surgery."

"How long was surgery?"

"Five hours."

"Oh, God, what did Dr. Brooks have to do?"

"Your intestines are back together. I'll tell you the details when you're not so sedated."

"How are you, Muff?"

"I'm exhausted."

"Will I need more blood?"

"One more unit."

"That will be number eighteen. Why do I need all this blood."

"In performing the surgery, a large vein in your abdomen was nicked and you bled. A vascular surgeon was called in to close it."

"Oh, God, a really close call."

"Get some rest. I'll stay with you a while."

Too anxious to sleep I want to fight back and be strong. But I'm too fatigued to open my eyes. I speak softly, "Thank you, babe, for all your love . . . I'll make it . . . we're a team."

"Are you comfortable?" she asks.

"I'm fine. Nothing hurts."

I awaken during the night when nurses enter to hang another unit of blood. Martha has left. The red-haired nurse named Barbara takes my temperature, blood pressure, and pulse, checks the dressing, and measures the output of urine. The pressurized stockings on my legs used to help prevent blood clots are regularly pumping and collapsing. They annoy me. "Please take them off or turn them off."

"I'll turn them off for a while."

I hope she will forget to turn them on again.

I listen to her read the numbers on the blood unit to the other nurse. She starts the blood flowing through the PICC line into my heart. "Thanks, Barbara, I appreciate your help."

I must receive the blood or I'll die. I know that I could die from either the AIDS or hepatitis viruses that may be in the blood transfusion. As a surgeon, I used to tell my patients they had a one in three-thousand chance of contracting hepatitis or a one in thirty-thousand chance of getting AIDS from transfusions. I would give them these statistics without concern for their fears. I'll be sensitive to those fears if I practice again.

DAY ONE HUNDRED TWENTY-SIX

FRESH WATER

I awaken at six on this sixth morning since surgery. The IV fluids run slowly into me. Yesterday, the tube to my stomach was removed from my left nostril. My nose and throat ache. I reach with my right hand and push gently on my abdomen. It's soft. No swelling has occurred overnight. Nothing hurts. I seem stable, making good progress.

Sunlight streaks through the open curtains. I say prayers and hope for water—maybe cranberry juice and custard. I wonder if my taste buds work. What sensations will I have swallowing? What will happen inside me? I hope for the best, swallowing small amounts and maybe passing gas. But, if I bloat or become distended the NG tube will again be inserted in my nose. Oh, I hope not.

At exactly six-thirty, the chief surgical resident and intern knock and enter. The intern, a thin, intense young man asks, "How are you doing?"

"I feel OK."

He sits on my bed and quickly pulls the sheet down and the johnny up. He rests his cold stethoscope on the upper, then lower abdominal quadrants and, with his head bowed, he listens. Then, speaking to my bandages and drains, he reports, "There are some bowel sounds." Looking up at the chief resident he continues, "I think liquids can be started." The resident nods. Then, looking at me, says, "You can have water today."

During the five-hour operation less than a week ago the perforation was patched, parts of the intestine connected in a Y-configuration, and the J-tube site closed. I hope it will hold together. Is it too soon to test it?

"How much water will I get?" I ask the resident.

"Two tablespoons every three hours."

I am amazed that it will be so little. "I think I can handle it."

The intern rises from my bed and he and the resident leave.

As a gynecologist-obstetrician, I, too, sat on the foot of my patients' beds. I remember a time in my first year of practice sitting with Dodie, a thirty-seven-year-old raven-haired woman, five days after her abdominal hysterectomy and removal of her ovaries. "Dodie," I said. "I plan to send you home tomorrow. You are doing well. Your blood count is good. Let me check your incision . . . It's healing well." I then looked at her face. "The report of the tissues, the path report, shows that the tumor in your left ovary is not completely normal. It's not cancer. It's called a grade-zero tumor. If it were a cancer it would be called a grade I, II, or III. Both of your ovaries were removed because of the growths in them. Only the left had a grade-zero growth."

"What should I do?" Dodie asked me.

"Have a consultation with a gynecologic oncologist. Have the slides of the tissue reviewed and discuss management. Grade-zero tumors of the type that you have don't require chemotherapy or radiation. I can arrange for the consultation at Johns Hopkins in about two weeks."

"Will you explain this to Carlos?" she asked, referring to her husband.

"I'll be glad to. Can he be here this afternoon at five or so?"

"Yes, I think so."

"If I had a grade-zero tumor, an "almost" cancer, I wouldn't be worried." I said and left.

Now I wonder, how much did that reassure her? She had the unknown before her, as I do now.

DAY ONE HUNDRED THIRTY

RESURRECTION

The sun wakes me and I listen to my slow, unlabored breathing. I hear no humming motors, no beeping alarms. No fluids run into me. Comfortable and calm, I wonder about eating breakfast—maybe Special K and banana slices.

First to the toilet, then, standing at the sink, I examine my sunken-but-bright eyes and the mostly gray stubble that surrounds my neat, thin beard. After washing and shaving, I wet my sparse, straight head hairs and comb them. I smile. I am alive and sort of handsome.

Picking the best shirt and pants from the closet in my hospital room, I dress and slip into loafers for the first time in months. I feel good enough to leave the hospital and go with Martha to the family Easter celebration. But, can I go? Can I get a pass? Will I be strong enough to sit up for the drive and to eat dinner? I want to celebrate being able to eat and being part of the family.

After two days of liquids, this morning's breakfast tray has real food: cranberry juice, a banana, and cereal with milk. I sit in the bedside chair with the tray in front of me on the small rolling table. Bringing the juice to my lips, I sip, taste the cranberries, then swallow. I feel the cold go down my throat into my chest and then my stomach. I listen— no sounds from my gut. Slicing the banana onto the cereal, I pause before eating. What will happen when I eat it? Chewing a spoonful of banana and Special K, I swallow, then wait. Nothing. No pain. No strange noises. No sensation. No cramps. No gas.

After four spoonfuls I feel full and stop.

Lilies perfume the room with spring's aroma. Approaching the bed, I step out of the loafers and lie down dressed. My energy is fully spent.

Martha's morning call wakes me. "Hi darling, how was your night?"

"Fine. I've eaten breakfast and feel great...and I'm all dressed!" I say brightly.

"You're doing so well. You really ate solid food?"

"Yep. And no gastrocolic reflex." This body reflex causes the urge to defecate while or just after eating. "How are you?"

"Fine. I'm leaving for Tom and Cathy's now."

Do I have the courage to ask my doctors if I can leave the hospital to go with her? Tears fill my eyes and then stream silently down my cheeks. Aching with sadness, I know I cannot go. I can't get out, even for a short visit. I feel sad, isolated, and angry. Covering the mouthpiece, I weep.

"Are you okay? You're not saying anything."

"I . . . was . . . hoping . . . I . . . could . . . go . . ., too."

"Oh, darling you are crying. I can't stand it, you being alone and crying. I'll come over now and then go to Weston. I love you so much. I wish you could go."

"No, you go . . . I'll be all right. I'm . . . just . . . so . . . tired . . . of being . . . sick."

"What a lot you've been through."

"You go. I'm okay."

"You sure? I'll come over now."

"You go."

"I love you so much. And, Chris and Titia are coming to see you at one o'clock," she reminded me.

"I love you, babe. See you this afternoon."

With gladness for having my wife, I feel the cool tear lines drying. I roll onto my right side, close my wet eyes and try to see myself at future family gatherings: Martha's birthday in May, Fourth of July in Bristol, Thanksgiving at the cabin, Christmas at the big house in Providence.

A few hours later, gentle knocking announces my friends Titia and Chris. "Hello," Titia lilts brightly, her face radiant with energy and happiness.

Chris smiles, "Hi, buddy."

"Happy Easter!" She hands budding forsythia branches to me and kisses my right cheek and then my left. Chris beams as he holds my hand in his. "You seem better, stronger," he says

"I am. I'm eating solid food with no problems. Had a meatball and some spaghetti for lunch."

Titia's happy eyes catch mine and, looking at her face, I wonder what my mother's face would be like if she were here. If alive, my mother, Thelma, would be eighty. Titia, in her sixties, looks wonderful and smiles easily. "I cut forsythia for you from the south side of the barn and crocuses are pushing through the snow there, too." Titia and Chris' only daughter, Joan, died from breast cancer at twenty-nine and is buried in this south-facing memorial garden. My mother died during my internship year. I wonder if flowers are blooming around her grave as well.

"How was your trip here?" I ask.

Chris answers, "Easy. About two hours and with little traffic—due to the holiday, I suppose. Tell us about you."

"It's April and I've been thinking about my favorite holiday, April Fool's Day."

I tell them that, when my children were in school, I came home early one April Fools Day to trick Dan, then a high school junior. He had tickets to his first concert by the rock band U2. As I sat in the living room waiting for him, I saw him open the front door. "Hi, Dan," I said.

"Hi, daddy-o, what's happenin'?"

"I've got some bad news... Bono (the U2 lead singer) is in the emergency room and has appendicitis."

"No! That can't be!" Dan's eyes widened in shock and filled with angry tears. He would miss his first U2 concert.

"Do you know who will be operating on him?" I ask.

"Dr. Tort?"

"No. April Fools."

Laughing with relief, Dan asked, "He's really okay?

"Yes, he's really okay." I assured him.

Chuckling at my story, Chris and Titia grin.

Looking at them I ask, "May I tell one more?"

"Sure," they say genially.

I tell them that in the early nineties I was the chairman of a hospital committee investigating a physician allegedly performing too many operations. Meeting weekly for four months, the physician members of the committee, the hospital's general counsel, and the medical staff coordinator attended to every detail dictated by the professional staff by-laws. In March, the final report was presented to the medical staff executive committee. A presentation to the professional committee of the board of trustees was planned for April 10. On April Fool's Day, I asked my secretary to call the hospital president's office and tell his secretary that I could not continue on the committee because of pressing personal matters. She placed the call and moments later the hospital president, called back.

"Al, this is Vic. What's come up? You've done months of work. You can't quit now. We'll have to start all over. And, what's this personal matter?"

"I have to spend time with a friend."

"Who?"

"April Fool."

Laughing, "You got me. I'll get you back!" he said.

As Titia and Chris rise preparing to leave, I turn and point to the window and ask, "Do you see the daisy bouquet next to the Easter lily? That's from Vic. We're still friends."

Standing near the bed, I embrace both of my dear, dear friends.

The following morning, Easter Monday, a card from a New Hampshire friend arrived with a poem I placed in my journal:

Long, long, long ago;
Way before this winter's snow
First fell upon these weathered fields;
I used to sit and watch and feel
And dream of how the spring would be,
When through the winter's stormy sea
She'd raise her green and growing head,
Her warmth would resurrect the dead.

Long before this winter's snow
I dreamt of this day's sunny glow
And thought somehow my pain would pass
With winter's pain, and peace like grass
Would simply grow. The pain's not gone.
It's still as cold and hard and long
As lonely pain has ever been,
It cuts so deep and far within.

Long before this winter's snow
I ran from pain, looked high and low
For some fast way to get around
Its hurt and cold. I'd have found,
If I had looked at what was there,
That things don't follow fast or fair.
That life goes on, and times do change,
And grass does grow despite life's pains.

Long before this winter's snow
I thought that this day's sunny glow,
The smiling children and growing things
And flowers bright were brought by spring.
Now, I know the sun does shine,
That children smile, and from the dark, cold, grime
A flower comes. It groans, yet sings,
And through its pain, its peace begins.

— Mary Ann Bernard, *Resurrection*

PART THREE

PART THREE

DAY ONE HUNDRED THIRTY-TWO

A BOMB

Sitting on the toilet, I wait. I feel the rectal pressure that persuaded me to leave my hospital bed. I wonder, is this really an urge to go? It's been months, actually last year since I had the urge to go and had a bowel movement. How long shall I sit? How can I know? Holding my breath I gently bear down. Nothing changes. I think about what I've eaten: a banana, some cereal, one meat ball, scrambled eggs, pea soup, pound cake, and peaches. I try imaging my muscles relaxing. I wait for a movement to start. No change. Maybe tomorrow. I'm tired of sitting. I try another tactic. I support my abdomen with my hands and bear down more forcibly. Feeling a strong urge, I push harder. and hear a splash.

"Bombs away!" I declare. Then, standing, I look down at the stool of a seven year old. I am proud of my work and return to bed.

DAY ONE HUNDRED THIRTY-THREE

HOME PORT

On this ninth morning since surgery, I anxiously await the doctors' visits. Will I be discharged? Am I ready to go? Will my intestines continue to work? Will I regain the weight I've lost? How long will it take? I look at my hands, so thin the translucent skin reveals the outline of the bones.

The chief surgical resident greets me with "Good morning" and sits down on the bed. He inspects the healing incision and drain sites. He removes the staples and carefully tosses them and the staple remover into the trash can. With a puzzled look he pauses, then brings his thumbs near a slightly swollen area in the scar.

As his thumbs press together on the swollen area, I gently grasp and pinch his left ear between my right thumb and forefinger, not wanting him to force the infection deeper. "We're not going to hurt each other, are we?" I say respectfully. He withdraws his thumbs with a mild grin.

"You may have a stitch abscess there," he says.

"I saw that—what shall I do? I'm supposed to go home today."

"Every four hours apply warm compresses for fifteen minutes, wash with peroxide, and then apply gentamycin ointment and a dry dressing. If you can probe it, use Q-tips with peroxide."

Another bump in the road. So many bumps to this trip.

Later in the morning, Dr. Banks, the giant, visits on this departure day he predicted months ago. He smiles and his eyes sparkle. "You're doing well. Remember to eat. Even if you're not very hungry, always eat the meat. You need it."

"Should I take vitamins?"

"You can take a multivitamin if you wish."

"Any particular brand?"

"It doesn't matter."

"Will my hair grow back?"

"It may." He pauses. "I'll see you when you're next here seeing Dr. Brooks." I extend my frail hand. He shakes it kindly.

"Thanks, Dr. Banks."

No vitamins? I guess the intestine will absorb what it needs. Then I remember a colleague's quip: "The dumbest intestine is smarter than the smartest doctor."

At ten-thirty Dr. Brooks makes his morning visit. Wearing a white coat over scrubs and green rubber clogs, he stands tall, smiles, and comfortably crosses his arms on his chest. During this odyssey he has seen me daily except for a very few days he has been away. His eyes smile as he says, "You can go home today."

"I'm really going!" I exclaim.

"Fred told me about your incision. Let me take a look." He carefully loosens the tape and gently folds back the gauze. He inspects it and says, "This is superficial. Please call me if the drainage soaks the dressing. I'd like to see you in two weeks."

As he replaces the bandage, I slowly exhale the breath I've been holding. "I'll make an appointment, and, Dr. Brooks, I want to thank you for all your care." His face expresses his appreciation.

In the reclined front seat I sleep most of the drive home. Snow patches cover some of the front walk so we enter through the garage. Up eight steps to the first landing and I stop. Martha brings a chair and I rest. Then, up eight more and into our bedroom.

Home at last.

My ship is now in harbor;
Its sails are furled,
And gentle waves
Make peaceful murmurings
Along the shore

My friends are here to greet me
And to tell
Of what is closest to their hearts
Now that the journey of the week is o'er.

Tomorrow I shall once more set the sails
And head again for an uncertain sea,
But I shall have a compass and a star
And vision that this hour has given me.

— Benjamin R. Burdsall, *In Meeting*

DAY ONE HUNDRED THIRTY-FOUR

PROTECTION

This morning I awake to the wind whistling in the birch trees. Through the skylight I see sunlit wisps of white clouds race across the sapphire sky. Martha sleeps by my side. On the bureau the forsythia branches have burst with butter-yellow blossoms.

Silently I pray the Lord's Prayer and then remember an intensely lonely evening when I was sixteen.

Lying on my bed at Harvey and Helen's farm, feeling empty and isolated, I sang The Lord's Prayer and began to weep, then sob. I felt the comfort of God's presence.

Another memory comes . . . I was being tossed about in a narrow bunk while sailing through an Atlantic Ocean storm when I was forty-one years old.. I recited this same prayer continuously to calm myself until I fell asleep.

"Holy Spirit, You protect and cherish my essence. The power of Your love is greater than all human suffering . . . including mine."

DAY ONE HUNDRED FIFTY-FIVE

LIMITED VISIBILITY

K nowing my journey thus far and the uncertain course to my future, I feel perplexed. A dense fog covers the ending of the critical phase of the illness and the beginning of recovery. My weakened body needs strengthening and my posture needs improvement. My skin needs repair and I want to grow hair.

Today I begin physical therapy for the third time during this illness. In a cubicle in the therapy department, Anne, the physical therapist, advises, "Stand tall, think tall."

With effort I straighten up, pushing my chest up and out and pulling my shoulders back. I tense my abdominal muscles. "Ouch."

"Where do you hurt?" Anne asks.

"My incision. My abdomen." The pain passes and I relax.

"Let's go to the exercise mat." I lie on my back and she asks me to do ten leg lifts with each leg. I do seven with the left leg, nine with the right. Then, holding a one-pound weight in each hand, I lift them over my chest. She wants ten repetitions but gets six with my left arm, eight with my right. As I finish, sweat beads up on my forehead. My arms shake and shudder. "Rest a few minutes," Anne tells me. "Then you can go."

While resting, I review the session and my status. I tolerate climbing one flight of stairs now. When will I do two? I can walk a block. Will I ever walk a mile? Two? Three? Performing the work of rehabilitation, I trust the fog will lift. Yet, every time I cough or sneeze, the upper part of the incision bulges and hurts. I have incisional hernias. I need an operation, my fourth in this year of illness. I want a healthy body, but I am so tired of beginning again.

At home, I read this prayer from my worn copy of Ted Loder's *Guerrillas of Grace*:

Help me believe in beginnings
God of history and of my heart,
So much has happened to me during these whirlwind days . . .

You know my frail heart . . .
Oh God, help me to believe in beginnings
And in my beginning again
No matter how often I've failed before.

Help me to make beginnings
To begin going out of my weary mind
Into fresh dreams
Daring to make my own bold tracks in the land of now . . .

Help me to believe in beginnings
To make a beginning
To be a beginning
So that I may not just grow old
But grow new
Each day of this wild, amazing life.

REFITTING

During the weeks following discharge from the hospital in Boston, I go to physical therapy on Mondays, Wednesdays, and Thursdays. Anne, the "stand-tall–think-tall" therapist, manages my program of strengthening and improving the range of motion of my spine and joints. She also assigns home exercise. I use a twenty-four-inch ball under my abdomen and chest for support when exercising my neck, back, arms, and legs. By the third week, I drive myself the eight miles into town for appointments. Using one- and two-pound weights and riding a stationary bicycle, I am gaining strength.

At home after exercise I take a daily "beauty rest," sleeping soundly for two hours or more. Today, awakening in the den, I walk slowly to the hallway past the framed photo collages of our family's first twenty years. Dressed in swimsuits, costumes, ski clothes, and both formal and casual clothing, family and friends from infants to grandparents fill this gallery of celebratory moments. Faces look at me from homes and travel locales in Williamsburg, Virginia; Bethany Beach, Delaware; Alaska; Colorado; and Mexico. I pause and study the richness of those years, then head toward my bedroom.

I step through the bedroom doorway and as my bare foot touches the carpet, I hear a calm, gentle voice say, "Life goes forward."

Alone in the house, it can only be the still small voice from within. "Yes, life goes forward," I agree.

That evening lying in bed, Martha takes my hands in hers. "Your hands are stronger."

"They are."

She takes my wedding band from her necklace and places it on my ring finger. It fits.

NEW COURSE

In May 1999, Martha and I travel to New York City to see Dan's senior thesis film, *Traffic Jam*, and attend his graduation. We celebrate the end of his ten-year voyage.

In June, Martha takes me to Bermuda for rest and relaxation. The two-and-a half-hour flight reassured us of a prompt return to Boston for emergency medical care, if needed. Staying in a cottage on Cambridge Beaches, we enjoyed fragrant tropical flowers, spectacular vistas, and gourmet dining. It is a time together in paradise.

In July, a retired physician friend named Harvey drove from Maryland to visit me in New Hampshire. Having him as a colleague was one of my great professional fortunes. As we cared for patients, served on the hospital's credentials committee, and provided leadership for the county medical society, his knowledge, integrity, and wisdom inspired me to do my best and be my best. One of his beliefs is, "I treat people with trust and honesty and expect them to treat me the same way. If they don't, I move on." I, too, believe this.

Stepping down from the cab of his one-ton, red diesel B.A.T. (Big-Ass Truck), he spoke as the proud son of Waycross, Georgia, that he is. "Ale, ah needed to see ya. Ah want ya to know ya have a future." We embraced.

A week later as I drove to Boston for a monthly appointment with Dr. Gregory, I wondered what my future would be. Granted a one-year leave of absence from work in February, I am regaining my health. The incisional hernias will be repaired in September. How long will recuperation and rehabilitation take? When will I be strong enough to work? To operate? To take night calls? At this point in my life I feel too fragile emotionally to practice, even if I were physically able.

Sitting with Dr. Gregory in his hospital office and looking at his tanned face and gentle smile, I sense his willingness to have me begin. "Since the last time," I say, "I've been thinking about your question—what are my unfulfilled adult goals? First, as a person, I want to explore my creativity and spirituality."

I use notes to continue. "As a spouse I want to dance, to travel, and to deepen our relationship. As a father and member of our extended family, I want to invest in my children and relatives as they permit."

Sitting up straighter, I resume, "I value friends. I want to be intentional about having friendships. I want to serve others. Since the days of my medical internship, I've been guided by a Quaker advice: 'The service to which we are called requires a healthy body, well-trained mind, high ideals, and an understanding of the meaning and purposes of God.' I want to support efforts that relieve suffering. I want to help provide opportunities for education and personal development for others and myself. I'd like to write about this illness experience."

I pause and sigh. "As a physician, my unfulfilled goals are . . .," I hesitate. ". . .I'd like to write about what I learned and the mistakes I made as a clinician and teacher—perhaps call it *The Pearls and Pitfalls of a Clinical Gynecologist*."

Sighing deeply with relief, I continue, "I might teach again. I don't know where . . . or when. I am grateful to be a physician. So much has fulfilled me: learning, teaching, helping others, solving problems, being needed and respected. These are the best parts. However, it is hard work at times. Practicing is so physically and emotionally demanding with long hours, lots of standing, being tied to a beeper or cell phone, calls during the night, and sometimes driving to the hospital while most others sleep. Sometimes I used to sweat bullets during and after a difficult surgery. A few of my best efforts resulted in adverse outcomes. Fortunately none were fatal. And, medical practice is now a business managed by insurance companies and government departments. Their goals and mine are so different. I want the best for patients, the insurance companies want the least and the cheapest . . . and they also want to control my efforts. They make practicing more difficult than it needs to be . . . than it was. Sometimes I think I have given what I could give to people and to medicine. I'm . . . finished . . . I think."

After a long pause he comments, "You still have the passion you had before becoming a physician."

Surprised by this information, I am also reassured. My body has taken a beating. I have physical and psychological scars. Yet, Dr. Gregory believes I still have my desires, motivations, aptitudes, and optimism— my spirit.

Leaving Boston I think, *What is my life about now?*

Driving north on Interstate 93, I see a bearded driver and think about Arthur, a bearded elf-like college drama professor who taught us the Stanislavsky acting method. During rehearsals on the Goddard Auditorium stage at Earlham College he asked us, "Who are you and where are you going?"

Now, life is the stage as I begin a new scene. During the more than one hundred and fifty days and nights of my illness, the best efforts of scores of nurses and other professionals from transportation aides to physicians and surgeons helped turn my tide toward healing. My family and friends' love and spiritual support, a divine companion, and Dr. Gregory's guidance all nurtured my psyche and spirit. I am alive and grateful.

Being is the now of becoming.
—W. Wilkinson, potter

SANDFLY POINT, NEW ZEALAND

February 25, 2002—On this warm, clear, late afternoon, Martha and I finish hiking the Milford Track. Exhilarated and exhausted by this four-day, thirty-three-mile effort, we have traversed primeval forests, the foggy granite summit of MacKinnon Pass, the three-thousand-foot descent along Arthur River's cascading waterfalls, and more. In the scars of floods and tree avalanches, the mosses, ferns, and trees root themselves on solid rock. Life renews itself.

Completing the track, I know greater physical strength and mental stamina than before my illness. My body functions seem normal for my age. However, my mouth goes dry and my pulse quickens whenever I enter a hospital, have blood tests, or a physical exam. But, this anxiety is lessening with time.

Occasionally the unresolvable issues of my illness interrupt my sleep. The questions—Why the adverse outcomes following the first surgery?, What if?, and If only . . . —now get little of my attention. In these predawn awakenings, I focus instead on my blessings: the human and divine love I know, the beauty of the earth, friends, and family, and, after eighteen blood transfusions, having no hepatitis or HIV. I have my health and the passions of my youth: to help others, to love, and to be loved.

The illness is over.

GRATITUDES

I am grateful for Titia Bozuwa, Sue Wheeler, and the Twin Farms Writers' Workshop Members, who guided my beginnings; for Don Benson, Elaine Buderer, Laurie K. Lewis, Don Link, Richard Lohaus, Paul C. Nicholson Jr., Martha Sherman, and others whose questions brought clarity to this effort; for Marcia Henderson and Judy Richardson for typing the manuscript; for Becky Rule for her guidance, wit, and wisdom on the road to publishing; and for my wife, Martha, whose encouragement and love have made this book and my life possible.

APPENDIX

ALLAN'S FOOD LIST

Root beer float
Peppermint ice cream with chocolate sauce
Banana split
French toast with maple syrup
Butter brickle ice cream
Rum raisin ice cream
Egg in a hole
Halibut fillet with hot mustard and pistachios
Fresh trout cooked by the stream
Smoked quail hors d'oeuvres
Butterscotch pudding
Tapioca with quince jelly
Single malt scotch
Melted brie and slivered almonds on gingersnaps
Cooked turnips
Canned pears
Leeche fruit
Rose duck
Lamb chops with mint sauce
Hamburger, lettuce, tomato with yellow mustard and catsup
Grilled Reuben sandwich
Asparagus rolled in ham
Pineapple upside down cake with melba sauce
Mount Gay Rum, tonic and nutmeg
Virgin Pina Colada
Ice cold chocolate milk made with Hershey's chocolate syrup
Meat loaf with ham and cheese layer
Fresh raspberry tart
Coconut ice cream
Coffee ice cream
Petite filet mignon

Borscht and dollops of plain yogurt or low-fat sour cream
Scones with Thursday Cottage lemon curd
Dry Sack sherry with lime
Blueberry buttermilk pancakes
Cherries Jubilee
Fresh Maryland steamed crabs in Old Bay
Blackberry cake with granular sugar and low-fat whipped cream
Hot fig newtons with ice cold milk
Fresh ice cold lemonade with vanilla wafers
Chinese summer salad from China Chef
Coho grilled hamburger
Raspberry pillow cookies
Pumpkin pie
Meat-free spinach lasagna—Dick Cahall's recipe
Cheesecake made with low-fat cottage cheese
Root beer Popsicle
Danish desert cherry pudding
Junket pudding
Hot chunky applesauce with fresh gingersnaps
Vanilla Coke
Cherry Coke
Old-fashioned glazed donuts
Meatball sub
Turkey breast sandwich on 7-grain bread with cranberry chutney and lettuce
Lunch at Brew Moon in Boston
Chocolate mint cookies with French vanilla ice cream
Hermit cookies with warm milk
Very, very thin slices of fruit cake with low-fat cream cheese
Yellow ribbon candy-lemon
Chocolate meringue, French vanilla ice cream and raspberry sauce
Ritz crackers with peanut butter
Hot mulled cider, cinnamon stick and sour cranberries
Barbecued chicken Baboli with asparagus
Barbecued beef or pork Baboli with green peppers
Fruit fondue with dark chocolate sauce
Beef fondue in broth, horseradish and mustard sauces and baby red potatoes

Fresca
German chocolate cake and ice cold milk
Watermelon, lightly salted
Steamed Mussels in white wine, garlic and fresh shallots
Boston cream pie
Austrian hot dogs in split green pea soup
Jarlsberg cheese and dry white wine
Cheese fondue, Swiss style
Walrus blubber, garlic clove and black bread
Fresh Muir eggs over whole grain rice
Sun tea with peanut butter cookies
Iced peppermint tea and orange cookies
Almond cookies with fresh pineapple pieces
Chocolate ice cream in waffle cone with pineapple sauce
Yogurt covered pretzels with fresh strawberries
Lobster and corn on the cob
Oysters wrapped in prosciutto topped with champagne pistachio sauce
Fresh cantaloupe
Raisin oatmeal cookies
Cucumber salad with fresh chives and lemon mayo
Apple slices with cheddar cheese
Pretzels